LIFE IS A GAMBLE

A Memoir

By

Dee Shaw

To:
Radmila
Best wishes
with love
Dee x

All photographs were provided by the author.

ISBN:978-0-9993116-7-7

Published by Early Girl Enterprises, LLC United States

Dedication

I dedicate this book to my wonderful husband, David,
whose love has turned my life around and to my beloved
son, David.
I love you both.

Acknowledgments

Enormous thanks to the army of magnificent people who made this book happen: my son David, husband Dave, brother Radovan and Caroline Kuzmanovic, Daniela O'Donnell, Hansa Bakhai, Sanja Bjelica Simeunovic and Tamara Simeunovic, and Heracles and Blagorodna Economides. Without your consistent, compassionate support, my life wouldn't be the same today.

My son, David, encouraged me to write and publish my story, so without him, this book would simply not exist.

Thank you to Una Carnigie, Kate O'Rigan, Jackie Drury, Ian Griffin, Jo Spencer and the wonderful Management Team at Highgate Mental Health Centre. You were the best and most supportive colleagues I ever had through my entire career.

I feel so fortunate to have found Peter O'Connor of Bespoke Book Covers. We worked seamlessly together to create this stunning book cover.

Lorna Lee was my beautiful editor who worked tirelessly to turn my rough draft into this book. Always positive, kind, and accommodating, Lorna goes the extra mile to help authors. As a first-time author, I was concerned about finding the right support for this ambitious undertaking. I feel I hit the jackpot when I was introduced to Lorna. I whole-heartedly thank Lorna for her expertise, advice, and hard work that she has put into editing my book. I appreciate all that Lorna did to bring this project to fruition. I would recommend Lorna 100% to other authors. You will struggle to find someone as honest and professional as this gifted editor.

Finally, my thanks to England for welcoming me as an immigrant all those years ago and making me one of your own. This country has given me an opportunity to better myself and give something back to British society by helping others to overcome their difficult times.

Note to Readers

I was born 1949 in Serbia, the former Yugoslavia, and from a very early age, I cheated death. This book is about me, my parents, and my siblings. My life's journey has been tumultuous, but I've never stopped struggling for a better life. By the time I was 20 years old, I had realised that there were no professional or personal opportunities for me in my native country, so I decided to strike out on my own to achieve my dreams, but in a foreign country where I didn't know the language.

My goals were simple: to live an independent life and be a respected member of my community by working hard and being financially responsible. I wanted to be safe, comfortable, and happy, too. While these may not seem to be lofty goals to many people, living a life like that was (and is) the ideal for me. And the only way for me to achieve my goals was to never give up on myself or my dreams. To use a well-worn expression, I played the cards I was dealt with the best of my ability.

This narrative covers six decades of my life in chronological order and represents my best recollections of my experiences of the events that (and people who) shaped my often-troublesome journey. I used only the first names of significant people. In many cases, I fictionalised those names for privacy purposes. The names of towns and cities are real. Because of the political upheaval that took place in my country and the eventual dissolution of Yugoslavia in the early 1990s, I refer to Serbia as my country of origin throughout this book.

I don't know if courage and resilience is an inborn trait or is cultivated over a lifetime of facing daunting challenges and surviving them. However, I know now that I have an inner strength compelling me to share with you both the obstacles I faced and the rewards I experienced by embracing life in a positive, proactive way. I hope you'll find my story both powerful and inspirational. If by reading it, you find your inner power or inner voice, then my life will have been all the more meaningful.

Chapter 1

My Beautiful Perunika (Iris)

My name is Dee, the Westernised version of my given Serbian name: Dragica. During the 1950s and early 1960s, I lived in Serbia with my parents and three brothers and two sisters. We lived in the rural countryside on the outskirts of Perunika. The village was named after the Iris flower.

Perunika was a beautiful village surrounded by acres of corn and other vegetables and picturesque meadows sprinkled with red, yellow, and purple flowers. Perunika was also known for its hills, green grass and beautiful streams.

In the summer, looking after the crops kept most of the people in our village busy. After the autumn harvest, it was time to get ready for the winter. The winters were social times. People would meet at each other's houses to share meals, stories and enjoy themselves.

During the evening, women would weave bedding and clothing for their families; they also crafted intricate, beautiful embroidery. They did not have radios or televisions available, so they would entertain each other by telling jokes or singing country songs. Men would play cards, drink a local drink called slivovica (plum brandy), and tell jokes to each other. By this time, the children would be fast asleep in bed.

I often think how lucky I was to be raised in such a pretty place with many friends and brothers and sisters whose company I enjoyed immensely. There was an uncomplicated contentedness about my life back then that I sorely miss. But not everything about my life in Perunika, Serbia was idyllic.

My original family home (photograph taken many years after I had left).

My parents had three boys and three girls; I was the youngest of the girls. We were very poor. We had very few clothes to wear. Hunger was a routine part of life. Most of the time we lived on vegetables harvested by my parents. We rarely had bread made of wheat flour. If we ate bread, it was baked from corn flour, which always seemed hard and dry. I hated it.

My brothers and sisters and I would complain, but my mother said, 'Eat your bread and be grateful. At least you have bread. Many of our friends haven't had bread for weeks!'

It was hard for me to understand this at the time, but food rations applied to everyone in the village after the Second World War.

From time to time, my father would go to a small town called Kurshumlia, which was about ten to fifteen km away from our home. If he was lucky enough to have something to sell (like the odd chicken or some vegetables), he would be able to buy most of the essentials (like salt, sugar and cooking oil) with that money. But sometimes he brought home a special treat. When my dad would buy a loaf of white bread that was baked from wheat flour, still slightly warm, the aroma was unmistakable. To this day, the smell of fresh-baked bread takes me back to our little home. We'd sit on one of two large, rough-hewn benches skirting each side of the sturdy but uneven wooden table that my grandfather made. Then our usually perfect manners disappeared. Mum tried to stop us from greedily reaching across each other and the large table, but even her batting our hands away wouldn't stop our frantic efforts to seize a morsel of that soft, aromatic delicacy. We excitedly fought each other to reach my father's hands for a piece of that exquisite white bread. Often several of us would tumble to the floor in the process. We fell off those benches like apples fell off a tree in late autumn.

One loaf of white bread didn't go far with six children and two adults, but we were grateful to be able to have even a small piece. I could see my father's face – how proud he was at that moment – but, at the same time, I could see the sadness in his eyes.

After everyone settled down, I asked my mother, 'Why is Daddy looking so sad?'

She replied, 'He is sad because he is not able to give you children more and provide a better life for you all.'

'But Daddy is a good Daddy,' I protested.

'I know he is, Dragica. He wants to do more for us. This is not for you to worry about. 'Her tone told me not to ask any more questions.

Later I would learn that my father promised my mother that he would do something about our poverty. He would leave home to search for a job with wages. Unfortunately, his plans were derailed…for a while.

Tragedy befell our family. I had a nasty accident at the age of four. From then on, our problems only worsened.

Life is a Gamble

Chapter 2

Cheating Death at Four-Years-Old

In September 1953, my parents were harvesting corn ten to fifteen minutes away from our home. They were close enough to see our house from where they were working. While my mother transported corn by cattle cart, my father stayed on the farm to harvest more corn and prepare it for my mother to take home and unload.

I was left in the house with my older siblings; my two sisters and brother were only five, nine and ten at the time. On that fateful day, my mother, bless her, unloaded corn from the cart and left the cattle cart on the hill unattended, ready to go back to collect more corn. She decided to go in the house to make sure that we were all right.

While in the house, someone shouted to my mother and said that a baby calf had run out of the stable. My mum left us in the house and went to look for the calf to bring it back to the stable. While she was chasing it, I left the house unnoticed and jumped on the empty cattle cart. At the age of four, the cart looked more like something to play on than a piece of farm equipment. I placed my right foot on the top of a large metal nail that connected two carts.

Cattle cart similar to the one I jumped on.

At the time, I probably thought I was going to have a fun ride. I had a ride, but it wasn't fun for anyone. The moment I jumped on, the cart began to move. Fast! The cows were being bitten by flies, and they went berserk, pulling the cart behind them down the hill with me in the tow. Half of my little body was on the cart, and the other half of me was hanging off, my head dangling just off the floor like a rag doll.

I started screaming.

My mother must have heard the screams and came running towards where she'd left the cattle cart, but it wasn't there.

I don't remember any of this, but my parents told me that the skin at the back of my right foot got caught on that large metal nail, pulling most of the flesh off my foot. When I was taken off the cart, approximately ten to twelve cm of flesh from my foot was hanging off. My father and his friends rushed me to the only hospital in a tiny town ten to fifteen km away from our home to see the surgeon– the only orthopaedic surgeon in the whole region.

I don't remember much about the accident, but I have a vague memory of being under the big walnut tree behind our house, surrounded by many villagers who came to see what happened and, I guess, to support my parents. My poor mother felt responsible, guilty and distraught. She said she was in shock at the time, and that she would not forget the trauma that we all experienced as a family until I fully recovered.

My foot was severely damaged. In those days, there were no experienced orthopaedic surgeons to deal with that sort of intricate surgery. It would have been much better if the damaged flesh was put back where it had come from to provide me with some cushioning under my foot. Unfortunately for me, the surgeon simply cut off the dangling skin. The surgeon lacked specialised training and experience to handle my type of injury because he was both a general practitioner and orthopaedic surgeon. It was easier for him to get a pair of scissors and cut my skin off.

My father took me to him every day to clean and bandage my wound. After a short time, my foot developed gangrene. The surgeon suggested that my foot be amputated. My father's emotions swung from utter sorrow for his little girl to infuriation at the surgeon who couldn't fix her.

In those days, there was a stigma attached to having a disabled child. Having a daughter who was also an amputee would be embarrassing for my father and rest of the family.

My father made a drastic decision and told the surgeon, 'I cannot cope with bringing up a disabled child. 'His jaw muscles were tight, and he kept opening and closing his fists. I could tell that Dad was angry. The next thing he said left no doubt in my little-girl mind that my father was upset. 'If you go ahead with amputating my daughter's foot, I will shoot you first. Then I will shoot her and then myself! I will not be able to see a daughter of mine hopping around for rest of her life without being able to walk. 'In those days, there were no artificial limbs that could be fitted. My father loved me very much, but he was a proud man. Even then, I understood. But I was afraid.

To avoid this triple tragedy, my father took me back to the village and decided the family would look after me. He felt the best chance to save my foot was to have people who love me tending to me. What a caring and remarkable human being my darling father was. He made his decision not to bring me back for further treatment. Picking up his lame little girl, we left the hospital. He made his way back to the village with me in his arms.

On the way back, he became panicked. My father admitted that he was scared about the decision that he just had made. 'What if your foot gets worse? We do not have any training in how to care for a wound such as this. If we make it worse, it will have to be amputated anyway.'

Fortunately for him (and me), when he got back home, he called most of his friends and neighbours to our house to ask them for help. Sure enough, most of them came as there were not too many in the village to start with. They rallied round my father with their own ideas. It was collectively decided that my foot should be cleaned, treated with alternative medicine and bandaged daily. They did not have any medical bandages; instead, they used rough cotton sheeting that my mother had weaved herself.

According to my parents, this procedure was carried out every day for weeks and weeks. When my wound started to heal, cleaning and bandaging was slowly decreased to every other day for a good while, and then once a week until my foot was fully recovered and completely dry. My parents and my older siblings were always protective towards me, keeping a watchful eye on my foot at all times.

It took two years before I could walk again. In those days, there were no crutches that I could use for support. I probably wouldn't have been able to use them properly anyway because I was so young. As a result, I had to rely on my parents or my two elder sisters to get me off the bed to a chair or from here to there. They also taught me to hop.

By then I was almost six-years-old. My foot had fully recovered and was completely dry. My father decided to take me back to the surgeon to let him have a look and to see what he thought about my fully-recovered foot. I think Dad also wanted to show him how I could put my foot on the floor without any fear and managed to walk slowly.

Unaided. The surgeon was amazed and congratulated my father on his bravery, courage and talent. 'Now that the wound is bone dry,' the surgeon told Dad, 'it needs to stay like that, and it should be okay. 'My dad nodded, but I know he already knew everything he had been told. Nevertheless, my father was pleased with the doctor's feedback. Dad thanked him and took me back to the village.

When we got back home, my father invited the people who helped and supported us to our house to let them know about our visit to the surgeon and to thank them for their constant support. He told them, 'Without you and your support, my little girl might not have recovered so well from that horrible accident, and it might not be as happy an ending as it is.'

I do not remember anything about what had been done to my foot other than what my parents told me. Two of my dad's friends came by regularly to take my dressing off and change it. Because I knew how painful that procedure was, I would be frightened and scream my little head off every time I saw them. I would even grab my mother's skirt and refuse to let go. My dad always had to pull me away from my mother. Later, I found out that both parents felt so sorry for me that they both secretly cried after each time they saw me distressed.

When my foot was well enough to have physiotherapy, one of those helpers had the genius idea to get old dried corn cobs and gently roll my foot forward and backward over them. That's how the physiotherapy was done. My father told me the whole story when I was old enough to understand what went on with my foot, how they all coped during those two years after the accident, and how he saved my foot from being amputated.

Getting my foot to the point where I could start physiotherapy took a long time. Being able to stand, walk, or run took even longer. While I was grateful that I knew my foot was improving, I was frustrated that I couldn't move about like a 'normal' child. My slow recovery –or my appearance as a child with a serious disability – meant that my parents wouldn't let me attend school. I was a curious child and longed to fill my head with knowledge about everything from the history of my county to why the stars twinkled. But all I learned as a girl was how to do domestic chores while my foot healed, and I relearned to walk normally.

For the first 20 years of my life, I had no suitable cushioning under my foot. When I came to the UK and learned some English, I visited specialist surgeon at a London foot hospital for a consultation and was told to leave my wound alone while it was nicely dry. They also provided me with a soft insole to wear under my foot. After six decades, I'm pleased to say that my foot is still fine and functioning properly.

My dad is my hero; he was an amazing human being. I am so grateful to my parents for what they have done for me, especially to my father for saving my foot. I told my parents many times after my accident how lucky I felt to be alive. I promised them that, when I grew up, I would look after them.

And I did – financially – from the first month I arrived in the UK (in 1971) and for the next three decades.

Life is a Gamble

Chapter 3

My Dad, The Miner

When I fully recovered from my injury, my father was free to realise his dream of lifting his family out of poverty. He left home to work hard to provide a better life for all of us. He went to work in a mine 300 km away from our home, leaving my mother on our small farm with a few animals to look after and six children to raise (between two and twelve years of age).

She had to work from dawn to dusk. We hardly saw her during the day. My two older sisters were eleven and twelve and were able to help, so their experience of that time was different from mine. They hardly played with their friends once Dad left. Besides working with Mum on our farm, my sisters also worked for other people just to earn a bag of wheat so we didn't starve. I feel sad for them because they missed out on the freedom and joy that is supposed to come with childhood.

One of my sisters, Milka, was affected quite badly by having to work so hard at such a young age. I noticed that she was paler, thinner, and quieter than usual. And her smile had disappeared. I asked her, 'Milka, what's wrong? Are you sad about something?'

She sighed as she took my hand. I noticed how raw and cracked her skin was. My eyes widened when I caught a peek of some bruises on her arms as her sleeves rode up when she reached out to me.

She noticed and pulled her sleeves down. 'Dragica, please don't tell Dad...or anyone. We need the money, and I don't want to complain.'

I nodded. I would do anything for my sister. 'But, Milka, how did you get those–'

Milka shook her head. 'Sometimes I don't work fast enough. I do the housework and take care of the farm animals. If I don't get to everything, they punish me. 'She spoke with her head bent down.

'By hitting you?'

Milka nodded just once. 'And they make me stay longer. I'm so tired, Dragica. 'Her voice cracked.

I hugged her. She clung to me for a long time.

I kept her secret but worried about my dear sister's health. Not long after our conversation, Milka seemed to get worse – soul-sick and almost grey in pallor. One evening she didn't come home. We found out that she had run away to our aunt's house to seek refuge. When Mum and Dad found out why, they brought her back home, My mother found it very difficult to stay in the village by herself even with my two teenage sisters helping as much as they could. There was just too much for her to do. Before my father left home to find work, both sisters looked after the younger siblings (including me) while my parents laboured on the farm. As a single parent, all of the parenting, household, and farm responsibilities fell on her shoulders alone. She was always tired. All she wanted to do after a gruelling day of labour was to go to bed and sleep, but that was not possible. She still needed to milk the cows and feed the dog and the chickens. When she finally made it into the house, she needed to prepare food for all of us. My two eldest sisters were still young but working hard elsewhere. They were just as tired as Mum. When they got home, they couldn't face more drudgery. Instead, they went to bed – many evenings without any food.

My mother became exhausted, unhappy and bitter that my father left her to fend for herself and look after us all, too, even though she agreed that he should leave for this new job. When she was around us, she would snap at us for seemingly insignificant things like not moving quickly enough when she asked us to do something. I often heard her blame my dad for her bad mood. Because her feelings were obvious, we all felt her pain (in our own ways) and became unhappy, too. I missed my Daddy so much but knew that if he didn't go to work and bring some money in, we would have starved and lived like paupers. He was gone out of necessity, not desire.

A year later, my father had an accident in the Maine mine and was buried under the coal. He sustained significant injuries – broken ribs – but he was lucky to be alive. My mother had no money to travel 300 km alone (or with her children) to visit my injured father. I was miserable with worry that he might not survive and that I may never see him again. I felt entirely helpless. My dad saved my foot from being amputated. I wanted to help him as he helped me. But I was only six-years-old, so I did the only thing I could think of to do. I prayed. 'Please God, make my daddy well and bring him home safe to us.'

My six-year-old faith wasn't as comforting as I hoped it would be. I cried for days, fearing that I would not see my dad again as he was so ill. All I wished for was to be next to him and to help him get better in the same way that he'd helped me with my injury. But I was as helpless as a little bird with broken wings. All I could do was pray for him and wait until he came home one day. If he came home…

My dad was in hospital for three months. None of us visited him during that time, not even my mother. He wrote to my mother to tell us how he was getting on, so I knew he was alive; that gave me some relief. In the last letter, at the end of those three months, he told Mum that he was getting better and hoped to be out of the hospital soon. As soon as he was allowed to leave, he said he would come home to visit us.

My prayers were finally answered one day in the middle of the night when we were woken up by our mother shouting to tell us the good news. 'Children, children!' She called. 'Wake up! Daddy is home!'

I woke up crying, thinking I was dreaming. Then I saw my dad. I was so happy that I cried and cried for joy, thinking how lucky I was to have my daddy back with us, safe and well.

That night was one of the happiest moments I can remember as a child. My father was granted one-month sick leave. During that time, my mother managed to persuade him not to go back to work so far away from home. We all supported her request by pleading with him to listen to Mum and get a job near us.

'If you get a job closer to home,' my oldest sister said to Dad, 'you can help Mum on the farm. At least on the weekends.'

Dad nodded thoughtfully. Mum sighed, her rough hands gently straightening her discoloured apron.

My other sister chimed in. 'Yes, Dad. Anyone looking at Mum can tell she's been working too hard and can't carry on by herself much longer.'

'And neither can we!' My older sister added.

My father looked at my mother. Although she didn't return his gaze, I saw him smile lovingly at her and then at the rest of us. I could tell that he would try to help his beloved family financially without being absent from his home. If there was a way, he would find it and make it work.

My father found a solution, but it was far from ideal. He got transferred to another mine closer to home. There was no transport available from his work to the village where we lived. There was no easy way for my father to travel home for weekly visits. He had to walk forty-five km each way, regardless of the weather. Because of the love he had for his family, nothing stopped him from coming home each weekend. Despite how awful we all felt about him leaving home each weekend, we were thrilled to see him again at the end of the week. I'm sure he felt the same emotional push and pull.

The wages that my father received were so low that they only covered food to feed us. Clothes and shoes were given to us by the Red Cross. My father had no proper winter shoes or clothes. I remember he was always freezing when he arrived home. It was hard for me to see my parents struggle as much as they did. I wanted to make Mum's life easier so that maybe she wouldn't be so tired and moody all of the time, and Dad was too kind and loving a person to suffer so much. I just didn't know how to help either of them.

My dad was often unwell due to the lack of warm clothing. When he would travel during the winter, I hardly recognised him as he would come through the door covered with ice and snow. It was so hard to see him in such a state, but he was always positive and had a smile on his face. Dad's unfailing optimism helped me not to be too worried about him when he would arrive home for the weekends.

As a child, I remember not having many of the basic necessities of life (like food and proper clothes), my nasty accident, my dad's accident in the mine, and my mother's depression and exhaustion without my father being around to help and support her with us children and the farm. My mother became angry and resentful towards my dad and the six of us children, too, because Dad was leaving us all again and she had to look after six children and work on the farm by herself all week with little help from my two sisters. The rest of us were too young to be anything but burdens to Mum.

Mum and Dad later in life. Dad always had that smile.

While I was growing up, I always felt closer to my father than my mother even though he was away so much of the time. Why? Partly because of what my dad did for me after my accident and partly because he was more affectionate than my mother. My mother's childhood was unhappy. Her parents were very strict, and she was often beaten by her parents, especially by her mother. I believe that's why she was quick to anger with us children and had a negative outlook on life in general. I did not feel particularly loved by my mother while growing up, something I didn't understand until I was in my 20s, but I always loved her because she was my mum. And during those precious times when she was happy, she had a heart of pure gold. Unfortunately, she wasn't happy very often due to constant pressures and a hard life.

I guess I learned from my parents how to be tough. They taught me from the early age to work hard, never to spend more than I earn, and not to expect handouts. In those days, no one had enough for themselves, let alone extras to give to others, so handouts weren't even possible.

We had to be strong in every sense of the word. Our survival depended on it. And it wasn't just being emotionally resilient or accepting hunger as normal or quietly making do that toughened us up. We lived across from a seriously disturbed man: my uncle who had a vendetta against my parents.

Chapter 4

The Dangerous Uncle Next Door

There was a serious problem in the immediate family: a land inheritance dispute between my dad and his brother. My uncle intensely objected to the way my grandfather had equally divided up his land between his two sons. My uncle wanted more land, than his father left to him. As a result of that dispute, my dad and his brother's relationship was irreversibly broken. My uncle became very angry with both of my parents and began acting out against them in unpredictable and bizarre ways. I'm sure this is another reason why Mum was upset with my dad when he took the mining job. He was leaving us knowing that his unhinged, wrathful brother was living near us and that this man was a constant threat to us all.

My uncle lived a short distance opposite our house and wasn't just upset about not getting the land he thought he deserved. He was jealous of my father's ambition, too. Many times, he would work himself up and confront my dad with vile, nasty remark hoping to provoke an argument or fist fight. He used to wait for my dad when he came home very late at night and no one was around. He would throw stones at Dad or physically attack him.

My unhinged, wrathful uncle.

As I was growing up, I saw my father a few times with a swollen face from attacks by his own brother. My uncle was a bitter and twisted man whose rage was easily fuelled by his equally hateful wife. She, too, felt unjustly treated by my grandfather (and us) in the land deal and wanted to make our lives miserable.

The minute my father went back to work, my mother and we children became vulnerable. Mum was threatened by both my father's brother and some villagers who were also jealous about my father's desire to provide a better life for his family. My father was always hard-working, positive and lived in the hope that life would get better one day. It did get better, but it was a long journey for all of us to travel for a better, happier life. And along the way, these relatives and neighbours were trying to bring us down for having a dream and trying to achieve it.

While my dad was away working, my uncle was constantly abusive and threatening to my mother, telling her to leave the village with her children and to go away with her husband. He'd say, 'I don't want you here, and one day I will take all the land from you.'

My madman uncle would come to our house at night when all the villagers were asleep and BANG! BANG! BANG! on the front door trying to break in.

Mum would say in a harsh whisper, 'Shush. Do not cry or yell at him. It is just too risky.'

'Why?' I often whimpered into my mother's ear as I clung to her neck, absolutely petrified. The fear never ebbed.

'It will just encourage him to come after us. He wants us to be scared.'

I always startled when he would bellow, 'Come out, or I will break the door.'

This scene played out time and time again. We were too scared to cry. My uncle never broke the door down, but each time that he was banging on our front door, we were terrorised. We had many sleepless nights because of his threats. There was something truly sick about that man.

The situation got so awful that my mother used to keep a metal crowbar inside our house by the door in case he did break in so she could defend herself and her children. As it was too risky for us to go out at night, my mother kept a chamber pot made of clay in the house for us to use at night if we needed to go to the toilet. In those days, toilets were outside and away from the house.

The threats didn't stop there. I heard my uncle say more than once, 'I will kill you and drink your blood! And there won't be anyone to protect you because your husband is too high and mighty to stay on the farm. 'There was something wild – something crazy – in his eyes when he would talk this way. My mother became afraid of my uncle and what he might do to her and Dad. Poor Mum. She was battling all these fierce emotions: fearing my crazy uncle, resenting Dad for leaving her alone to handle everything, struggling with daily exhaustion and frustration, and yet admiring her husband for trying to provide for his family.

My mother was right to be frightened of my uncle. One wintery, snowy morning, he tried to kill her. Fortunately, he failed. I was always worried about my mother's safety. I believed that one day that my beast of an uncle would kill her and all of us; this had a huge impact on me as a child. I was always clinging to my mother and had many sleepless nights imagining that this would be the night he would break the front door to our house and kill us all.

The scary thing was also that there were no other houses nearby as most of the houses in that village were scattered far from each other. No one would have heard anything or found us until it was too late.

On that winter morning, the snow was one-meter high, if not higher. My mother had to get up as early as5am to be the first in the queue at the mill to get flour. Before she left, she needed to feed the cows and put a sack of wheat on the sledge to be milled. The mill was six km away from our home by the river Toplica.

I will never forget this. I was about ten-years-old. As soon as my mother lit the gas lamp in our house, my uncle's house lit up, too. I could feel it in my bones: he was getting ready to carry out his threat to kill Mum.

My mother kissed us and said, 'I'll see you at midday. As soon as I get back, I will bake the bread that you all like for lunch. Be good to each other. 'Then she left.

Snow was still falling. We could hardly see her when she left, and I was so worried for her safety. Perhaps if my crazy uncle hadn't put the lights on in his house, I would have thought that he was sleeping, and my mother would be safe. But because the lights were on, I became concerned. My sisters and brothers were awake by then, and none of us went back to bed as we were so worried about our poor mother and what that wretched man might have planned.

By late afternoon there was no sign of my mother. I feared the worst. It was approximately 6 or 7 pm and dark outside. My two elder sisters, Milka and Zivka, who were just thirteen and fourteen at the time, looked at the rest of us children and started to cry. We were all frightened for our mum and for ourselves. Being on our own, that despicable man could easily come to our house and hurt us, too.

It was so quiet in the house that you could hear the flame in the glass lamp flicker. I looked at the window, and all I could see was a white blanket of snow and plump snowflakes coming down fast. I heard an old lady from the village below our house calling my two sisters' names. She then said, 'The cows with the sledge are here. Where is your poor mother? Did that bastard manage to get her?'

I suspect that most people in the village knew that my uncle had a vendetta towards Mum and wanted her dead. At that point, I forgot about being hungry. All I wanted was our mum to be back home safe.

My two sisters went down into the village to fetch the cows with a bag of UN-milled wheat on the sledge. The rest of us just cuddled each other, crying inconsolably. We believed we would never see our mum alive again. I felt so helpless. What choice did any of us have but wait for our mother or wait for the bad news? No child should go through such a dreadful situation, but we did.

About 9 pm, almost sixteen hours since we saw Mum walk away in the snow, two policemen brought my mother back home. We surrounded her, and our tears of fear were replaced by tears of relief. She was home and, as far as I could tell, unhurt.

A chorus of enthusiastic 'thank you' sentiments escorted the policemen out of our home. After the officers left, my mother explained what had happened. She said when she left the house, pulling the cows' reins in the deep snow, halfway to the mill, she spotted my uncle at some considerable distance but wasn't sure it was him until he got closer. 'The maniac was carrying an axe in his hand!' Mum wrapped her arms tightly round herself as if to form armour covering her heart and stomach.

He shouted at her, 'Now I will chop you into pieces and drink your blood, and I will make sure no one will ever find you.

When my mother realised it was him, she abandoned the cows, running for her life up and down snowy hills and falling into the potholes. Distressed and frightened, my mother eventually ran into the arms of a total stranger passing by and kept saying, 'He is coming! He is coming to kill me! He's going to kill me!'

'Who? The stranger asked.

My mother was terrified and badly shaken, but she managed to tell this man, 'My brother-in-law.'

The man who helped my mother told her, 'Don't worry. If he comes near us, I will deal with him. 'He quickly showed my mother a gun and said, 'If he comes near, I will shoot him.'

I told my mother, 'There are nice men, nice people, in the world. This man was ready to risk his own life for you, Mum.'

My mother nodded. She continued to tell us what happened. 'This man, he took me to the police station in the small town and gave them a description of that crazy uncle of yours. He told them that he saw a man running toward me with an axe in his hands while I was hysterically calling for help. 'A shiver ran through her. Again, she hugged herself either in an attempt to get warm or to shield herself from the memory.

The stranger also told the police that when my deranged uncle saw him, he went away. But that gentleman gave the police a description of my uncle, and my mother confirmed that it was her husband's brother who was after her. My mother told us that he said to the police, 'I will be happy to be a witness or help in any way to bring this man to justice.'

While Mum and this kind stranger were at the police station, apparently my uncle was busy trying to establish an alibi. He went back to the village and visited a few neighbours to cover his footsteps and hide what he had been up to. If the case went to court, he wanted to have witnesses to say he was nowhere near the alleged attempted assault.

Because he behaved like a madman and tended to threaten and harass many people, most people in the village were fearful of him, too. For that reason, no one from the village reported his threatening behaviour before this incident with Mum. People simply steered clear of him when possible.

That nice, caring stranger supported my mother through the entire court case to make sure that my uncle didn't get away with what he set out to do, especially after he tried to get an alibi back home from the neighbours. All I can say today is 'thank you' to that lovely man who was there at the right place and at the right time to save my mother. Unfortunately, none of us were able to meet this man and thank him in person for saving our mother's life. We were very young at the time, and he lived further away in another village. However, my father did meet him during the court hearing and thanked him. I will be forever grateful to him what he did for our mother and us, too.

Following a police investigation, my uncle was arrested and taken to the police station. The following day he was charged with attempted murder and sent to prison for several months. When he was released from the prison, my uncle's grudge against my parents became worse than ever. My father was still working far away from home, and not too long after his brother was released from prison my mother asked her own brother for protection. He accompanied her to the mill during the night, thinking my uncle would not know where she was. Unfortunately, his hatred was a sick obsession. My uncle discreetly followed them. When my mother and her brother got to the mill, my dad's brother waited around the mill to make sure no one was around. My mother went out of the mill to get some logs for the open fire, and my father's brother, (my deranged uncle) stormed inside the mill and stabbed my mother's brother in the stomach and then ran away.

When my mother heard her brother screaming, she ran in. To her shock and horror, she found her brother on the floor bleeding heavily from his stomach. She took her thick scarf off her head and pressed it into his wound in an attempt to stop the bleeding. Then she tied it round him. My mother and her brother were lucky that a neighbour not far from the mill heard her screaming and ran to help them.

My mother's brother was taken to hospital and saved thanks to my mother's quick thinking. She used her scarf as a tourniquet by putting it round her brother's stomach to stop him bleeding to death until they arrived at hospital. Following that horrifying, life-threatening incident, my dad's brother was re-arrested and sent back to prison.

My mother was very close to her brother. She told us, 'If my brother passed away and left his three children behind, my life won't be worth of living.'

She visited her brother in the hospital on a weekly basis. My mother was badly traumatised by seeing her brother in a pool of blood, so close to dying. She was also traumatised remembering what could have happened to her when my madman of an uncle tried to kill her.

My mother was so devastated by these events that she must have developed acute depression or some other emotional problem. She became very aggressive with her children and my dad, too. She was frightened to leave the house for a long time. My two older sisters, just young girls, cared for her. In those days, emotional instability of any kind was neither recognised as a valid medical condition nor socially acceptable. We all suffered as a result of her mental state and unusually antagonistic behaviour, as in those days there was no help available for mental health issues. Being so young, I didn't know what depression was, so I was confused. I felt she didn't love me anymore. I was scared for my siblings and me to be around her.

I remember waking up at night thinking what my mother was like before she became hostile and violent and how scared I was of our uncle. Now, I was just as frightened of my own mother. Dad was hardly ever around to remind me what love and joy felt like. Life seemed wretched all around. I had this thought more than once: *we would be better off dead than alive.*

While this self-destructive thought may seem extreme for a ten-year-old, I didn't conjure it up all by myself. I had heard my crazy uncle say it on many occasions, 'Taking someone's life means nothing. A stranger, a neighbour, a family member. It's all the same. When someone deserves to die, they need to die.' Even today, after six decades, I still get flashbacks. We were lucky to eventually get out of that village alive and create reasonably normal lives for ourselves.

Like hunger, being cold in the winter, and endless drudgery, violence (threatened or real) became a part of my childhood. I don't remember my mother hitting me. She beat up my two sisters and two of my brothers. Often. They couldn't do anything right in her eyes. My brothers and sisters were so angry and scared of her that they would just keep out of her way. Until they couldn't. I was different. When my mother was sad and angry, I was the only child who had enough courage, even though I was scared, to put my arms round her and tell her that I loved her. I was always clingy towards her no matter what, perhaps because I was as afraid to lose her as I was frightened by her behaviour. Whatever the reason, she still got upset with me but never beat me.

I wish the same were true for my siblings. They were so terrified of her. When she would stop beating them, my older brother would leave home and walk for hours to get to my father's sister who lived away in another village. There was no other way for him to get there but walk.

He would stay there in safety for a while, but when he was brought back, he would get another dose of beating for having left. Watching my darling brother being beaten in such a brutal way by our own mother and not being able to help him was very painful for me. I would often run to another room and curl up in a corner quietly crying. I was petrified that if she heard my voice, she would have gone after me, too.

As a child, I could not understand how she changed drastically from a typical, caring and loving mother to a monster without any feelings for her children. My mother's radical transformation affected me deeply. Watching the verbal and physical abuse was hard. I found it excruciating to be so powerless to stop the pain that everyone was feeling. As a result of constant aggression and violence in the house, I became a withdrawn and melancholy little girl.

When my mother told my dad what was happening with his brother and the escalation of the violence, Dad kept saying, 'It won't be too long before we will leave this place, leave everything and go.' And after three long years, he made his promise come true.

I'm not surprised that my mother had some kind of a breakdown. I didn't have any explanations for my mother's horrible behaviour towards her own family back then, but I do now. I understand what she went through while living in Perunika. It was awful for her to realise that she and her brother cheated death from her brother-in-law, but she did.

I'm pleased to say that many years after we left the village, my unhinged uncle finally died in the middle of a cold and brutal winter blizzard. He froze to death in 2013. He was alone and was dead for many days before he was discovered. I'll admit it: his death was, in my opinion, too merciful. For all the pain and suffering he wrought on my family alone, he deserved a slow, agonising demise. At least he was no longer a threat to me or anyone else. I found enormous comfort in knowing he was dead.

This may seem a harsh sentiment, and it is. I believe it's better to be kind than to be bitter or hateful, to be positive rather than negative. My father taught me that. We didn't want to harm him; we simply didn't want him to harm us. I applied this approach to many a confrontation in my life's journey.

And there were many opportunities along the way to practice this valuable lesson.

Chapter 5

Time to Move on to a Better Life

A couple of months before my uncle was released from prison for the second time, my parents often spoke about how worried they were about possible retaliation from him. They had enough day-to-day worries without living in constant fear of verbal or physical assault from my lunatic uncle.

One day, my dad gathered us round him. He told us that he and Mum had made a big decision. My dad said, 'I have got a new job as a security guard in the shoe factory in Blace. I will take you all out of this village forever and give you a better life. And you, Dragica, [meaning me] will be able to go to school there…hopefully.'

As a child, I had no choice in the matter: my parents said we were moving and that was that. I had my feelings about the move, however. One part of me regretted leaving the only home I had ever known (and all the familiar people) behind. The other part of me was excited as my father promised all of us a better life in our new home. Especially thrilling for me was that I could finally start my formal education at the late age of fourteen. Going to school and learning about everything I could meant the world to me.

In 1962, as Dad promised, we left the farm, the house, and the village I grew up in behind us. We all moved to a tiny town near Dad's new work. We had no accommodation to go to, no money other than what Dad was earning, which was just enough for food. There was no money to rent accommodation. In those days in Serbia; there wasn't any government help analogous to income support in the UK.

To this day, I don't know what my parents thought when they decided to leave Perunika with no home to go to. I suppose their priority at the time was our safety. It's understandable given what we had all been through up to that point.

The government offered my father meagre, two-room accommodation in a market building for one month only. In the middle was a weighbridge that was used once a week to weigh animals before they were sold. The room where we slept was used by one man. There was a chair in it to weigh bags of wheat and corn through the window. The weighing scale was placed outside the room under the window.

We were allowed to use this room six days a week. Every Tuesday was market day from 8am until 4pm. On that day, we all had to get out of this room for the whole day so we weren't in the way while the market was open. I was grateful that we were there during the summertime; otherwise, we would have been wet and cold all day. Hungry too. This was a humiliating time for all of us, especially for my parents.

Being a thirteen-year-old is a tumultuous time in one's life in the best of circumstances. I didn't have the luxury of indulging my personal moods or desires. I had more practical issues pressing on me. My family was in crisis – survival mode. We left everything and everyone we knew because we didn't feel safe in the only place we ever called 'home. 'I very much felt that we were refugees in our own country. We were forced to enter 'no man's land' and had nowhere else to go. We didn't even have a proper place to sleep. But I was grateful that we left our dangerous situation behind us and that, at last, we were together again with Mum and Dad.

Things slowly got better in Blace. My mum was able to make some supportive friends who helped her recover from her depression. Also, people in that little town gave us some old and worn clothes that you could almost see through, but we were grateful to have what they could spare as we badly needed any help anybody could give. The locals told us that they admired my parents for being strong and sticking with each other and their children no matter how hard it was. I was encouraged by their kindness.

From the time we left Perunika, my mother was desperately trying to get better from her depression. Smiles appeared more regularly on her face, making me feel happy and more secure being round her. I think my sisters and brothers felt the same. Eventually, she recovered quite well and became a loving and protective mother. But unfortunately, her anger and frustration that she had suffered during the time we lived in Perunika stayed with her until the end of her life. Poor mum. I'm deeply saddened that she had to go through such horrendous experiences and that she could never let go of the resentment she felt over it.

I admire my dad for having enough courage to leave everything behind and take us away from Perunika to a safer place. It was scary for him – the man who was supposed to protect and provide for us. He was the man of the house, but we had no house. He told me, 'Dragica, I do not know where we are all going to sleep on the first night, let alone for the rest of the nights we are here. But I *will* sort it all out. Do not worry. The important thing is that we are all together and safe. 'All he wanted to do is to keep us safe and get us away from his evil, dangerous and deranged brother.

We were all young children at the time aged between four and seventeen. To be uprooted so abruptly wasn't easy for any of us and our living situation was far from ideal. We were all sleeping in one room on two double mattresses. Mum slept with the three girls and dad with three boys. The pillows and mattresses were filled with hay that my mother prepared for us. It wasn't comfortable with hay sticking in your back in the night; our hair was full of it in the morning, too. It was prickly and messy.

But despite all this, when we woke up in the morning we were all so happy to be together. I choose to laugh at how funny we looked having our hair full of hay, bodies and faces scrunched to high heaven. But the only comfort that mattered was the comfort of togetherness in safety.

My mother cooked food and baked bread for us outside the building in the open fire since we had no stove. I was often embarrassed about how we lived at the time, feeling that we were living worse than travelling gipsies. In those days, only gipsies cooked outside.

Dad was able to get a job as a security guard for a shoe factory in Blace. My mother and two sisters, who by then were seventeen and eighteen, went with her every day to work on the government farm and did whatever they could to bring more money in.

My father was looking for a piece of land where he could somehow make a start to build something for us. To his surprise, there was a piece of land for sale next to the market building. The money that all four of them earned within a short time was not enough to buy that piece of land.

That didn't stop my incredible father. He may not have had 'book-smarts' (he only went to school until he was eleven-years-old), but my dad had loads of common sense. He was affable man who made friends easily. And he chose his friends wisely; they were supportive and knowledgeable. My father didn't suffer fools gladly. One of my dad's new friends lent Dad the money he was short of to buy this piece of land. Then this friend told my dad to ask the people who let us stay in the market building for a one-month extension. He did this, and it was granted.

My dad bought that piece of land. After he bought it, however, he discovered that he wasn't allowed to build anything on it. My father was devastated. Naturally, he felt that he had wasted money on it.

'Oh, no,' his friend said, 'I have an idea. 'Then he offered to help again. This friend told my dad he would get his friends to provide wood material and fill it up with mud mixed with straw, and they would help us to build one room to start with but that it would need to be built during the night when the neighbours were sleeping. He also told my dad that the government could come in the morning and pull it down.

'It is risky,' he told my dad. 'But the risk is worth taking. You cannot live like this with your family much longer, with no electricity, water or sanitation. However,' he continued, 'you can get away with keeping the building if you find picture of Marshall (the late president of former Yugoslavia) and hang it on one of the built walls.'

My dad went to a local school and borrowed one of the president's wall pictures and did what his friend advised him to do.

Sure enough, someone must have reported that there was a lot of banging going on and something like a shed looked as if it was being constructed on the land near the market. The officials from the local council came the next day and demanded my father take the picture down and destroy what he had built overnight. Because this happened during the communist regime, my dad's friend knew that if anyone removed the president's picture of the wall without the owner's permission, that act would be interpreted as an attack on government. The consequence? Imprisonment for the party who removed the picture. As my father was legally well-informed by his friend, he refused to remove the picture. The structure that would become our home remained intact.

When the local officials left, my dad let the dust settle down for a couple of weeks. Then he called his friends back to continue their mission, but this mission was different.

They prepared enough material again and brought in five of his friends who were professional builders. These men offered their labour free of charge to build a little room with the same material as first two rooms next to the one that was already built. The structure still looked more like a shed in the garden than a house. This would eventually be a bathroom and a little porch next to it, big enough for a single bed. The walls of these two rooms were made of mud mixed with straw.

The rooms were not even properly dried when we all moved in. The first room was big enough for two double beds, a table and a stove (donated to us for my mother to be able to cook and bake inside). My sisters and I slept together in one bed and the three boys together in another and mum and dad slept on the porch. From then on, Dad didn't have to leave the room anymore while my sisters and I were getting ready for bed. That was great.

We were all so happy, and I felt we had moved into a hotel, not that I knew what a hotel was or looked like. It was a small place, but it was ours. My parents saved enough money to put in a bath and build another two rooms. Those rooms were made of straw mixed with mud (like the others), but shaped into very large mud bricks, which were dried. Then the rooms were built using these 'bricks. 'My dad could not afford to buy proper bricks.

From then on, we three sisters had one bedroom to share – so did the boys – and Mum and Dad moved into that big room that was built first without planning permission. We used to call that room the 'lucky room' because my dad managed to save it from being pulled down by the government. At last, we had a comfortable place to live and sleep, but we had no hot water or electricity for a while.

At first, my father was denied electricity by the local authorities because he had built the house without planning permission. After many visits and constant persistence from my dad, he was eventually given a permit for electricity to be installed. Inside our house (for the first time in our lives), we had a proper bathroom and an inside toilet. What a luxury! Imagine my excitement to have electricity for the first time in my life at the age of fourteen (in 1963). That's a memory that never fades.

After a good while, there were two more plots of land for sale. One of my dad's dreams was to bestow the gift of property to each of his three sons when they grew up. He managed to buy two more pieces of land and held them for his sons. Because he assumed his daughters would find husbands to provide for us, he wasn't concerned about securing property for us. I understood then (as I do now) that he didn't love his daughters less; he was just from an era that thought differently about men and women. This extraordinary man put his children and their futures as his top priority. He was a family man to his core.

Eventually, we all flew the nest and left home except my middle sister Milka who is (and always will be) my special sister. To my surprise, that little house built of mud and straw is still standing after six decades. I visit it when I go to see my family in Serbia. Memories and emotions flood over me when I see that little house where I once lived – many pleasant, many not. One thing is clear, though: I feel that my hard and ill-fated upbringing made me a stronger person. I am today what my parents made of me. I will always be grateful to them for that.

If I hadn't had the challenges I faced as a young girl, I don't know how I would have coped with all the obstacles that were to come. And there were many.

Life is a Gamble

Chapter 6

The Oldest Student in Class

Due to my foot injury, I missed being formally educated. I was fourteen when we moved to Blace and still hadn't begun my education. After we settled down in this small and pretty place, my father went to the local school to speak to the headmaster and explain why I hadn't ever gone to school. He hoped to enrol me straightaway.

'Fourteen?' The headmaster scowled at Dad (he told me later). 'She is far too old. It is too late for your daughter to start school at such an advanced age. Impossible!'

The headmaster was right. But my dad knew how much it meant for me to be educated. He was very upset and worried about how to break the news to me. Since I was impatiently waiting for him to come home to tell me when I would be able to start my first day at school, he had to figure out a way to tell me.

When he walked through the door shaking his head, I knew the news wasn't good. Still, I had to ask. 'What did he say? When can I start?' Oh, there was such hope in my voice.

'I am so sorry, Dragica. The headmaster has denied our request. 'Dad's head was hung low. He didn't even look at me when he spoke.

I felt angry, wounded, and desperate all at the same time. But I knew that none of those feelings would help. I went up to my father and took his hands, almost forcing him to look at me. Standing as tall as I could, I took a deep breath and said, 'Dad, take me to the school so we can both see the headmaster. Maybe I can convince him to change his mind and let me start my schooling there.'

He shrugged. 'I do not think he will change his mind.'

'I want to try. Please, Dad?'

My father agreed to let me try.

I was nervous about facing the headmaster. When we arrived at the school, we were asked to wait outside the headmaster's office until he was ready to see us. While waiting for him, I kept thinking, *No, Mr Headmaster, you are not going to get your way! You didn't help my dad, but you will listen now. You will listen to me and help me out. You must!* I felt so frightened but was ready to put up a fight with him – whatever it took to get into the school.

He was an older gentleman. He lowered his glasses and said to my father, 'Why are you back? What did you not understand? Your daughter missed the boat. She is too old now to start schooling.'

How rude, I thought, *he shouldn't talk to my dad in that manner. And, hey! I'm right here! Don't speak as if I'm still at home. You won't get away without helping me, help that I desperately need. That's your job.*

My father was very embarrassed; he looked at me with a sad face and shrugged his shoulders.

I wasn't going to give in. I plucked up my courage. 'Please, please help me out. I want to learn how to read and write,' I said. 'I know I can be one of your best students. I'll work harder than any student you ever saw.'

'How are you going to do that?' he asked, with his arms folded tightly across his chest and his eyes narrowed.

I replied, 'I will read and learn day and night if I have to.'

To make him understand the reason I couldn't have gone to school at the right age and convince him of my toughness, I took off my shoe and showed him the scar on my foot. 'Sir, you are my last hope for a proper education and a normal life.'

The headmaster did not comment for a few minutes. He unfolded his arms and leaned forward on his desk. 'You are an incredible and very determined young lady. I am ready to help you out. Are you ready for this?'

I nodded my head and smiled. Dad did, too. Neither of us had any idea of what he was about to say.

'What I am proposing is that you study for six months. Then we will put you through exams. If you pass all the subjects, then you can go on to do the second year in the next six months. This means if you are determined and able to do that, then you can do two years of schooling in one. In four years, you can finish secondary school. Then you can go to college. Do you understand?'

I nodded.

'Good. Are you ready to start and see how it will go?'

My father looked at me, his eyebrows drawing together, and his forehead wrinkled, 'That seems like a great deal of work, Dragica. What do you think?'

I probably should have answered my father and addressed his obvious worries, but I didn't. I looked directly at the headmaster and replied, 'Yes sir. I'm ready. Thank you for the opportunity. I will do my best, I promise.'

The headmaster agreed to this arrangement.

I was so happy and excited, and I couldn't wait to tell the rest of my family the good news. When I did, they were all happy for me. Their joy and support delighted me, and I became even more determined than ever to start at that school. At last, I would be able to learn how to read and write. After the school holiday, I started my first day at school at the age of fourteen.

Being the eldest and the tallest in each classroom didn't bother me. What bothered me was that some children were cruel, and I was bullied. They taunted me with mean-spirited questions.

'Are you so thick that you have to keep repeating this class?'

'Can't you remember what you've learned?'

'How old are you, anyway? Did you wander into the wrong classroom because you're stupid?'

I was constantly bullied and picked on even though they were told from the start by the school authorities that I'd started my education as late as I did because I had a nasty accident as a child and it took a long time for me to recover from it. Some children didn't care. They were more interested in making my life as miserable as possible with constant bullying.

Children will always be children. It's a pity I didn't understand that at the time. They had conventional behaviour problems. Some of them were looking for a target, and that target, unfortunately, was me. My way of coping was to keep quiet and cry discreetly. The more I was bullied, the stronger I became. I never showed the bullies that I was bothered by their behaviour. All I was concerned with was how to achieve what I had promised to my parents (and, more so, to myself). I kept thinking how lucky I was to be given a chance for an education and how blessed I was to have such supportive parents and teachers. So, the bullies did not take priority in my life at the time even though it was tough. When they realised that they couldn't get to me, they moved to someone else to torment instead. From then on, I was able to concentrate on my school work instead of them, and I felt I was the winner in the end, not them. I moved on.

Teachers knew how much it meant for me to finish what I had started and gave me all the support they could; I did the rest. With willpower and determination, I managed to learn eight years of schooling in four years. I studied industriously and passed all my exams. Punctuation, grammar and vocabulary were my biggest challenges as there was so much to learn in such a short amount of time. It was not easy to achieve this, but I was very proud of myself. So was everyone else in my family.

During those four years, I was the talk of Blace. I was regarded as being a genius by many people, but I didn't think of myself as anyone special. I was an ordinary young lady who came from an unfortunate background. All I wanted was to improve myself and one way to accomplish that was through education. From a very young age, I knew what I *didn't* want, and that was more important than what I wanted. I didn't want to marry young, have many children and live in poverty.

When I finished secondary school, I begged my father to let me continue my education. My dream was to become a nurse. When I was fourteen, I was hospitalised for an operation on my appendix. I loved the crisp, clean uniforms of the nurses and the way they cared for patients. I wanted to dedicate my life to helping others in this noble profession. But I needed an advanced degree. This was not possible as I would have to go to live in another city. Unfortunately, my parents could not afford to support me financially. I was extremely disheartened, but I understood.

Life was hard for them at that time. They also had five other children to think about and support.

Instead of fulfilling my dream of continuing my education and becoming a nurse, for the next two years I worked on a government farm for minimum wage picking apples, strawberries and harvesting corn. It wasn't what I wanted to do for the rest of my life as it was seasonal, difficult labour, and I was the youngest of the workers. I could not cope with physical demands the job itself or the speed that was required of me to do the job up to their standards. Feeling sorry for myself, I spent many a day and night crying.

I received my first wages 48 years ago from that miserable job. It didn't pay very much (even by the standards back then), but I was thrilled to have my own money. I decided to spend some of the money to buy my family our first electric iron. Up to that point, we used an iron filled with hot wood charcoal because we never had electricity. You needed to be skilful to use an iron filled with charcoal not to burn the precious few clothes that you owned.

I was so proud bringing that electric iron in the house and showing it to everyone. *It's our first luxury*, I thought.

The expression on my father's face when he saw that lovely iron ended any joy or self-satisfaction I had in bestowing this gift. He was furious.

'How could you spend good money on *that*? We are still struggling to pay the bills to keep this roof over our head, and you throw away money?' He was shouting at me. Dad rarely shouted at anyone.

'But, Dad. I thought –'

He shook his head. He wouldn't even look at me. When he finally spoke, it was in a calmer, but unyielding voice. 'You take the iron back to the shop and get my money back. Now!'

I cried all the way to the shop, thinking, *I hope they won't take the iron back as it has been taken out of the box.*

I was right.

'I am sorry, Miss. It is store policy that we cannot accept merchandise that has been opened for a refund unless it is damaged or defective. Is there something wrong with it?' The shopkeeper asked.

I wanted to say, *Yes, there is something wrong with it. My father thinks it's a bad idea.* But I simply shook my head, no.

He pressed his lips together and shrugged. Then he said, 'My apologies for any inconvenience this may have caused you. There is nothing we can do.'

'I understand, Sir. Thank you.'

I left the shop with mixed emotions. I was delighted that my mum and my sisters would not burn clothes as we now had a proper, modern iron. But I was petrified to tell my father that 'his money' was not coming back to him. In the end, I was pleased that I was able to do this for my family and trusted that my father would realise that the iron was a good investment.

I always wanted to improve myself and do the right thing. But how to do that hasn't always been clear. My father's reaction to the electric iron surprised me, especially because I thought I was doing a good thing for my family. This was just the first of many experiences in which I attempted to follow my heart and code of ethics instilled by my wonderful parents but was either surprised, disappointed or appalled by the reactions of others.

Chapter 7

My Middle Sister's Serious Illness

After many bumps in the road, we settled in nicely in Blace, and my family was happy. Eventually, my middle sister, Milka, managed to get a job in the local knitwear factory as a manual worker. She was quickly promoted to a quality controller. During her fourth year on the job, she became very ill due to a failing kidney and was taken to a hospital 80km away from home. One of her kidneys was so bad that it could not be saved; she had to have an operation to have it removed. The doctors told my parents that my sister was so ill and weak that she might not pull through the procedure.

Milka had the operation and survived. She was in intensive care for six weeks. My mother was the only one who could go to visit her (and my dad from time to time). Because of our financial situation, none of the brothers or sisters could visit her.

Visiting days were Thursdays and Sundays for one hour only, regardless of her condition. My mother didn't have money to travel 90 km twice a week to visit her daughter. As it was summer, my mother slept on the hospital grounds instead of travelling back and forth for those two days to visit her daughter in hospital. Two weeks after the operation, doctors told my mother that they could not do anything more for my sister. 'She is very ill and has just a matter of days to live.'

I overheard my mother saying to my father and oldest sister, 'We need to call the priest to come to the hospital to give Milka's last rights. 'I heard her sniffling. When she continued, her voice was strained but soft. 'We need to…to prepare her clothes for…her…her burial.'

After some sobbing, I could not hear what else she had to say to them. I had to know what was happening to my beloved sister, so I just barged into the room crying and asked my parents, 'Did you say Milka is going to die?'

My dad said, 'She is very ill at the moment.'

My mother nodded while trying to dry the steady stream of tears washing over her face.

I was so frightened for my sister…and me. Losing her – never seeing her again – was inconceivable to me. I cried and cried. Then I looked up to the sky and said, 'Please God, don't do this to us. We've been through a lot in our lives. 'I pleaded with Him, 'Don't hurt us anymore. Please make my sister better.'

My father tried to calm me by saying, 'Try not to worry. Milka is getting better, and she will be okay.'

I only heard a sorrowful platitude from a grieving parent about to lose a child. I was sure that I was never going to see my sister alive again. I was devastated.

The next day, both my parents went to the hospital to arrange for my sister to be brought back home. To die at home.

My parents did not come home for two days. We didn't have a phone in the house, so they couldn't let us know what was happening. Those were long days of wondering and worrying about every worst-case scenario imaginable. I cried and cried for days. I couldn't eat and kept praying for my sister to be okay.

On the third day, my father returned home without my mum. He looked tired but relieved. 'Be happy, my children! Milka is showing signs of improvement. She must stay in hospital for the time being, but the doctors think she will recover.'

I didn't know whether to laugh or to cry. We all hugged each other while both laughing and crying at the miraculous news.

'Where's Mum?' Dragan, one of my brothers, asked.

'She will stay on the hospital grounds for the time being so that she can visit Milka and help her get better. I will stay here with you until it is time to bring your sister home for good. 'He smiled as he told us. It was delightful to see him smile.

I felt bad for my mum. As upset as I was about possibly losing my dear sister, she must have been devastated at the prospect and desperate for her child to get better. I'm sure it was difficult for my mother to cope with not being able to see Milka every day when my sister needed her the most. The hospital had strict rules about visiting patients that applied to everyone –one hour twice a week–regardless of how ill the patients were. The nurses were very good at enforcing the rules. She was not allowed to stay longer with my sister to hold her, love her and support her; these were important components to healing that Milka was denied. Mum told me, 'The nurses were so regimental. They had no compassion and, as far as they were concerned, the rules were the same for every visitor.'

It was hard for me no to be able to visit my sister in hospital. I wanted to hug her and tell her how much I loved her, but we were too poor to make even one trip.

Even without all the loving contact with her family, my sister had beaten the odds and got a little better every day. She was a determined and positive young lady. Within eight weeks, she had made sufficient progress and was allowed to come home.

The day my sister came home from the hospital I happened to be outside of the house. I heard some voices and looked to my left. I saw my sister! She looked very frail as she walked aided by both of my parents. They had travelled on the bus for over an hour. In those days, there was only one ambulance in Blace used only for life and death situations, so the bus was the only transport available to them.

My sister was almost carried by my parents as she could hardly walk from the bus station. She had lost a lot of weight. When I saw them, I just froze. Tears didn't even come (and I always cried easily in emotional situations). I suppose I simply couldn't believe she was home – alive – after so much time agonising about her untimely death.

When they put my sister to bed, I snuggled next to her, held her hand and stroked her face while whispering to her, 'I will never let you go anywhere from now on. I will look after you.'

She smiled at me. Her voice was barely audible, but she said, 'Thank you. I love you, too.'

To hear her talking and to have her back alive meant everything to me. Because we were so poor, no one in the family received gifts on Christmas, the New Year or birthdays. But if anyone had asked me what my biggest wish was, my answer would have been for my sister to remain well. I don't know if I ever told Milka that, but she was so determined to get better that, within six months, she was back on her feet and well enough to live a reasonably normal life.

My sister was steadfast in her desire to recover. I, too, am made of the same stuff. To make something out of myself in this life I've been given, I have had to remain positive and kind, keep a sensible, realistic outlook, and never give up when the going gets difficult. If my experiences in Perunika and Blace hadn't fully taught me this, I was about to get a crash course in building my character.

Chapter 8

My Long Struggle to A Better Life

In the summer of 1970, I was sent 280 km away by my parents to help my older sister, Zivka, with her two-year-old daughter while she was waiting to give birth to her second child, my beautiful niece, Svetlana. I was nineteen-years-old.

While I was there, a friend lent me a local magazine that had an article about a student organisation headquarter in Belgrade (the capital of former Yugoslavia) seeking young students for employment in London hotels as chambermaids or private, in-house au pairs. While this was not the kind of work I had in mind for my career, it seemed like a good opportunity to earn money, get some professional experience, and (perhaps most importantly) get away from the horrible crop-picking job.

I got so excited about the potential for a 'real job' that I wrote to them. Two weeks later, I had a reply. They asked me to bring my passport and go for an interview.

One of the interviewers asked, 'You have lived in Yugoslavia your whole life, yes?'

I nodded.

'Why, then, would you want to leave and take a job in England?' His pen hovered over his pad of paper, waiting to write my response.

I looked at his pen as I answered. 'I am one of six children from a poor family. With my minimum education, I won't be able to get a decent-paying job in Yugoslavia. My only qualifications are that I'm a hard worker, honest, and willing to do whatever I have to do to make my family proud. I also want to be proud of myself and make something of myself.'

Another interviewer on the panel asked, 'And you think working in England as a chambermaid will accomplish that for you?'

'Yes, Sir. If I can earn enough money to live a modest life and maybe send some money back to my family to help support them, too, that would make me very proud. But I need your help to get me in your program.'

The panel whispered among themselves for a short while. The one in the centre finally said, 'We believe you are the right kind of candidate for our program. Please leave your passport with us. We will sort out a working visa for you and send your passport back to you as soon as possible. Do you have any questions?'

I was so stunned that all I could do was shake my head. I didn't even say, *thank you!* After the interview, I had many questions, but it was too late. I suppose the important issue was decided: I was leaving my family and country to start an independent life in a foreign country as either a professional chambermaid or au pair.

Four weeks later, my passport arrived at my home address stamped with a working visa and a letter explaining that I would be travelling from Belgrade to London on January 3, 1971. Other young people who passed the interview would be accompanying me. The letter also explained that there would be someone from that company waiting for us at Belgrade airport to see us off and someone at London's Heathrow airport to meet us and take us to our posted assignments.

It all sounded organised and professional. I knew I would miss my beloved family, but I couldn't wait to leave my native country and start a new and better life for myself. I think my departure was harder on my family than it was on me. They were being left behind with the same old routines, minus me. I had nothing but exciting adventures awaiting me.

I arrived with my older brother, Zivoslav, at Belgrade airport and, understandably, he wanted to make sure that there were other students and that someone from the student organisation was there to see us off. To our surprise, no one from the organisation was waiting for me in Belgrade (or London) – students or officials. To this day I have no idea why. All I knew at the time was that I wasn't unduly worried that I would be travelling alone. I had a work visa in my passport and my darling brother to wave me off with a sweet, tearful goodbye. I was excited to go and didn't foresee any problems. I was a young, inexperienced and an innocent 20-year-old who was desperate to start my new life despite only having Yugoslav dinars equivalent to £5.00 in my pocket.

My attitude changed when I got on the plane. Panic set in when I realised that I was truly on my own. I asked myself the same question as my brother had when he waved goodbye to me, 'What if no one is waiting for you in London when you arrive?'

'Don't worry so much! I'll be all right.' I waved off his misgivings as if they were flies buzzing too close to my nose. 'The student organisation representative will surely be at London airport waiting, and they will take care of me. That's what they do!'

'Dragica, we're your family. We worry about you. That's what we do!' He hugged me tightly. 'We should contact them to make sure nothing has changed before you go.'

'That's silly. It's all been arranged. I'll be fine. You go home. When I get my first big pay check, I'll contact you. Then you can all stop your worrying. 'I wiped his tears away with my thumbs, and then I brushed mine away.

How oblivious and naïve I was! The gravity of my situation came crashing down on me as I sat buckled in my aeroplane seat. I was leaving a small country village to travel on my own to a big city in a foreign country without being able to speak or understand a word of their language. To make it even harder for myself, my parents could only borrow enough money for a one-way ticket to London. If even one thing went wrong, I was stuck with no money, no way to communicate, and no way to get back home.

On the plane, I sat next to a nice young Serbian girl. We started talking, as you do, and I told her that I was going to work in London. I showed her my passport along with the letter from the student organisation that included the name of the chain of hotels I would be working for.

'Will anyone be waiting for you when we land in London?' she asked.

I shrugged. 'I hope so, as no one from the organisation came to the airport to see me off. Now I'm concerned that no one will be waiting for me in London.'

She raised her eyebrows but didn't say anything. After a moment, she reached over and patted my hand as if to say, *everything will be all right.* Then she told me, 'I'll stay with you to make sure you aren't left stranded at Heathrow.'

Tears welled up in my eyes. I was taken aback by the kindness of this lovely stranger. 'Thank you so much!' I added silently, *Thank God for that.*

When we passed through passport control, I looked for someone with a banner from that student organisation. I saw no banner. No one was waiting for me, and no other students from the organisation were travelling with me on that plane. I was shocked. A feeling of dread descended on me.

The young lady that offered her companionship and help waited with me at Heathrow airport for about 40 minutes. When it seemed clear that no one would show up, I started to panic. I had no idea where to go, I had no money for transport and, most importantly, I was afraid of what could happen to me if that young lady left me. Because I was in such an agitated state, I can't remember what I said or did, but I probably started to cry.

Seeing that I was breaking down, she tried to calm me and assess the situation. 'Okay, I'm sure we can figure this out. Let's see. How much money do you have?'

When I showed her my paltry £5.00 in my pocket, I saw the horror on her face. She must have been wondering how anyone could let a young woman go abroad with so little money. I barely had enough money for one meal. Nothing more.

She said, 'Don't worry, as you have no money and don't know what hotel you are supposed to go to, I will take you to the head office of the hotels stated on your visa. They will be able to help you. 'She patted my back.

This young lady took charge of me, reassured me, and bought the travel ticket for both of us to go to my destination. When we got there, she stayed until another Serbian-speaking person was found. Then she wished me well and left.

Life is a Gamble

Quite honestly, I didn't understand what was happening. I wasn't even sure where I was, other than at the London airport, but I was relieved that this caring Serbian woman who spoke English didn't leave me on my own to figure things out myself. To this day, I often ask myself what would have happened to me, and where would I have ended up without any money and unable to speak English?

Because I was so worried about my safety, my instinct would have been to turn round and go back home. But I couldn't. I only had a one-way ticket. I was stuck, but at least I wasn't alone thanks to this kind woman. Even though she paid for my travel and took me to the West End to my supposed employer's head office, I still didn't know whether I was going to be okay. I left the airport with this woman who had been kind but was a stranger. *What if she's not what she seems? What if she's not taking me to the place she says she's taking me to? How will I know before it's too late? No one knows me here, and it seems as if no one is expecting me. I could disappear, and my family might not find out for weeks or months!* These nerve-wracking thoughts tumbled through my mind as we travelled on the underground, which was packed with commuters. I remained silent, looking around at a sea of unwelcoming faces, feeling sorry for myself. *Oh, my God, I thought. What have I gotten myself into?*

The condition of the underground transport system gave me an unexpected sense of relief. It was clean and pleasant – not at all like it is today. Many commuters were smartly dressed. Once we got off the train and exited the station via escalators, I could see that the staff had crisp uniforms. Walls were decorated with lovely pictures. The sound of pleasant guitar music was coming from somewhere. Some people raced past me; others took their time. Everyone seemed remote but polite. And no one spoke. If they talked, it was so quiet that you could hear a fly. I was fascinated by all this and felt as though I was watching a lovely fantasy film.

Then I remembered that I had no idea who I was with (other than that she was from my native country) and where she was taking me. It all seemed so bizarre and scary until we arrived at the hotel's company office in London's West End.

We arrived at the office at 3 pm. I was introduced to another Yugoslav woman. That's when my companion from the plane left me. I will never forget her or her kindness and generosity to me – a complete stranger. She helped me when I most needed someone to guide me through a confusing and desperate time. I truly wish I could find her one day and thank her properly from the bottom of my heart for being there. I would also love to let her know how I'm doing with both my working career and my private life. Without her, who knows what might have happened to me?

***

The Yugoslav woman from the central office immediately took control of my situation. She told me to wait for her to finish work at 5pm. Then she explained to me, as it was late on Friday, she wouldn't be able to take me to any of their hotels. 'The Head of Departments is off duty for the weekend. Once assigned to a hotel, you will be living there. Until then, I will take you to a youth hostel in High Street Kensington,' she explained.

'A youth hotel?' I tilted my head and bit my upper lip.

Her eyes widened. 'Not a hotel, a hostel. A temporary shelter for people who cannot afford regular housing.'

'Oh. 'I blushed. I had much to learn about life in the city.

When we arrived at the hostel, no other students were around. She introduced me to the housekeeper of the hostel who cleaned the place and cooked meals for students. The person who brought me there didn't tell me where I was supposed to go for my meals or that my meals would be free. She handed me a piece of paper with the address of where I should report to work on Monday morning. Then she left the hostel. I stayed there for three nights.

The last meal I'd eaten was on the plane on Friday morning. I didn't eat again until Sunday morning. As I couldn't speak any English, I couldn't ask anyone when and where in the building the food was served. On Sunday morning, one of the students put the clock hand on eight to tell me that breakfast would be served at that time and also demonstrated with her hands that I should go for breakfast with her.

I was timid but famished. I gobbled up my breakfast and left the dining room without putting the tray away. In those days, students were served meals, but they were expected to clear their trays and put them away. I was not aware of this, so I dashed back to the safety of my room. Soon I was called back by the cook who demonstrated how they remove the empty plate from the tray and put it in its designated place. My embarrassment only added to my homesickness. I was alone in a crowd, unable to communicate or share my feelings. Feeling sorry for myself, I went back to my room for the rest of the day without any food. I cried and thought, *why did I come to this country if I can't speak to anyone?* It was a bloody hard time.

To survive those early days, I had to give myself pep talks. I kept telling myself to keep going. *I came to London for a better life, and it's up to me to be strong, make a life for myself and make my parents and the rest of my family proud.* It's not easy to give yourself an inspirational pep talk when you're feeling miserable, but it's not only possible, it's vital.

On Monday, January 6, 1971, I left the hostel and put my best foot forward without looking back. I had no idea where to start or where to go, but I was moving forward. Although I had a working visa, I didn't know where the hotel in South Kensington was. I took my little suitcase with my few things in it and left the hostel feeling hungry, cold and weak. I said to myself, *oh boy, I will never forget this period of my life. No, I won't!* And I never have.

Life is a Gamble

When I was leaving Yugoslavia, my middle (and late) brother, Dragan, who was a policeman in Belgrade at the time, gave me a lecture before I left on how to look after myself and stay safe. He told me, 'Never go with anybody you don't know. Always ask older people or a policeman for directions and be aware of drugs. Oh, and never trust strangers.'

Fine advice, except, to me, everyone was a stranger, I didn't know who I should or shouldn't trust. But I had faith in God, and I prayed that He would protect me.

When I left the hostel, I kept hearing my brother's voice, 'Be careful, Dragica!' I got to Knightsbridge Underground Station with no money for transport and no idea how to get to the hotel I was supposed to work at. Taking a deep, shaky breath, I showed the letter and the name of the hotel to a complete stranger–an elderly gentleman. He bought me a train ticket and when the train stopped one station after Knightsbridge at South Kensington, that kind gentleman indicated by pointing his hands that I should exit the train. He continued his journey.

I was petrified as I didn't understand or know where I was or where I was going. Luckily, I got out at the correct exit – the same side as the hotel. When I left the station, I saw two young police officers. The hotel was very near South Kensington Underground Station, and they walked a short distance with me and pointed out the name of the hotel. I was so relieved and proud that I arrived at my destination safely.

When I enter the hotel, I showed the letter to the reception staff and was told to take a seat. Twenty minutes later, a member of the housekeeping staff, Helen, also from Serbia, came down to see me and took me to the staff quarters above the guest rooms in the hotel. She introduced me to chambermaids from my country. She said that they'd all look after me for the next two days until I met the Head Housekeeper who – at the time – had two days off. Her name was Bridget.

At that point, I felt safe and much happier as I was in the right place and was able to talk to some of my colleagues in my native language. *Great,* I thought, *at last, I've managed to arrive safe and well to my destination.*

When I met the Bridget with someone who spoke my language, she explained that I would be working for the rest of the day with one of the well-trained chambermaids who was also from Serbia. I was taken to Nina who was given the job of training me how to clean bedrooms, bathrooms and especially how to make the beds with hospital corners.

As Nina didn't like to clean bathrooms, I ended up cleaning them all day and didn't learn how to do the other jobs. The following day I was given six out of ten rooms to clean for Bridget to see what I had learned the previous day. As Head Housekeeper, she was testing me for speed and thoroughness.

I had never felt such pressure before. What would happen to me if I failed her test? I started to clean those rooms at 8 am and was supposed to have finished them by 4 pm at the latest. At 6 pm, I was still struggling to finish those six rooms.

As I hadn't returned to the office to sign out, Bridget came to see how I was doing and find out why I was still working that late. Her frown combined with her hands placed squarely on her hips while her foot aggressively tapped the floor told me that she was not happy with the work I'd done. Or not done.

During her inspection of those rooms, she found a dirty ashtray. She picked it up and threw it across the room. She kicked the waste paper bin across the bedroom, too. She pulled the sheets off the bed and made it properly.

'With hospital corners,' Bridget barked. 'As it is supposed to be done. Neat!'

I nodded, not knowing how to say, 'Yes Ma'am.' Even if I could tell my boss that Nina hadn't properly trained me on anything but cleaning toilets the day before, I wouldn't have. Bridget didn't seem like a person to accept excuses...only apologies if that.

No one sane had ever behaved like that in front of me. I was shocked and frightened at what she was doing, and I started crying. When she saw me crying, she got even angrier and walked out.

It took me another hour to finish those rooms. Bridget's assistant housekeeper came to re-check those rooms, passed them as clean and confirmed with Reception that they could be let to new guests. I was relieved that Bridget didn't return to re-check those unfinished rooms; otherwise, I probably would have been cleaning them all night.

My training troubles weren't over yet. Two weeks later, I received training with a different chambermaid on how to serve continental breakfast to hotel guests. She explained to me when and how to prepare the continental breakfast and at what time to serve each room. However, I was not told that I should start serving on my own at 7 am rather than waiting for an hour until my colleague arrived at 8am so that we could serve together.

I started work at 7am and sat in the pantry. At 8 am, I went to have my breakfast. Guests started calling the housekeeping office to complain that they hadn't received the breakfast they ordered the previous night, the breakfast they anticipated between 7 am and 8 am.

Following numerous complaints to the housekeeping office, the Head Housekeeper, Bridget, marched into the staff restaurant in the basement, shouting my maiden name, 'Miss Kuzmanovic!' She pointed her finger towards me signalling for me to come out. She walked up the stairs in front of me to the second floor and took me back to the pantry from where I was supposed to have been serving breakfast. Bridget showed me the breakfast list with the room numbers of guests who didn't receive their continental breakfast, all while shouting at me loudly.

I couldn't understand a word she was saying. Her tone and her red, grimaced face told me enough to be very worried about my job.

Bridget stabbed her finger at the breakfast list: the names of guests and the times people were scheduled to be served (all between 7 am and 8 am). Only then did I realise how and why she was so angry with me. When she saw me crying, she turned on her heel, stomped out and slammed the door. *The story of my life,* I thought.

I came to learn that Bridget was from Ireland. She had a thick Northern Irish accent, which made it even harder for me to understand her once I learned English. Standing only four-foot-six-inches tall, she always wore high heels. This woman was strict and fierce. I wasn't the only one frightened of her. Everyone who worked for her, and some who worked with her, did everything they could to stay out of her way. She kept many of us in constant fear for our jobs. Although I would never encourage this kind of leadership style, the woman was effective at maintaining a well-running, nearly immaculately clean hotel. She must have been doing something right.

Back in the 1970s, having a work visa for someone like me who didn't speak English meant nothing. Secure jobs were hard to find. For English speakers, losing a job wasn't the end of the world; it was fairly easy to find a new job within a week. For non-English speakers, the process of even searching for jobs advertised in English was impossible. Also, if the authorities discovered a foreigner wasn't working (even with a valid work visa), they could send you back to your country.

Losing my job at the hotel would have been disastrous. For all her gruffness, Bridget tolerated my language difficulties. So, whatever she asked of me, my answer was always, 'Yes, Bridget. 'Sometimes I understood what she was asking me to do; sometimes I didn't.

One day a guest requested an extra chair be delivered to his room. Bridget pointed her finger at a chair then towards the guest lift. What she should have done was put a room number on the chair to indicate the room number. If she had done that, I would have delivered the chair to the right place.

Instead, I took the chair and left it by the guest lift thinking, *if an elderly person waits for the lift, there will be a seat for them.* When the guest complained that they didn't get the chair and when she discovered where the chair was, she was very angry with me. Rather than recognising her failure to communicate adequately, she blamed me.

Bridget paced frantically between the interpreter and me. She finally blurted out, 'That girl is doing my head in! Does she do these things on purpose? I've had about all I can take from her!' The poor woman probably thought that I was completely daft.

After so many mistakes, Bridget was eventually happy with the rooms that I was cleaning. Through the interpreter, I requested to have ten permanent rooms in one corner of the floor area to avoid any misunderstanding. Bridget granted my request. From then on, I was much happier. So was she.

I worked at the hotel for nine months. During that time, I was able to find some house cleaning jobs during my one day off a week with Nina's help. My weekly wages from the hotel were only £8 per week (the equivalent of £98.75 per week in today's wages). I needed the extra money to send any cash I could to my parents. I was proud of myself that I was able to do that, and I definitely made my parents' lives a bit easier.

There were so many times in the early days of arriving in London when I had wished my plane ticket was a round-trip so that I could go back to Yugoslavia even though life over there was very hard. I would've lived in poverty with limited job opportunities and had no further educational opportunities due to my parents' financial difficulties. However, I have no regrets that my plane ticket was only one-way. I will never be ashamed of my humble and stormy beginnings in England. I achieved a great deal in just nine months. And I did it all through faith, sheer determination and a huge appetite for a better life because I didn't want to let myself (or anyone else) down.

But even the best intentions sometimes lead you astray.

Life is a Gamble

Chapter 9

Cheating Death Again in 1971

Twenty years after my harrowing accident on the cattle cart that could have ended in tragedy, I naively wandered into another – very different – situation that could have ended my life.

While working at the hotel, I became friendly with a female member of staff by the name of Nada. She worked in a different department but was from the same country as me. We spoke the same language, and she was always very friendly and caring towards me.

During our many conversations, she told me that she lived with her English boyfriend, John. 'He's so very nice. 'When she spoke of him, Nada had a dreamy look in her eyes. She even told me about their dog. 'We picked him out together. He's the loveliest dog I've ever known. '

They lived together in a flat not too far from the hotel. She kept asking me to visit her flat, meet her boyfriend and have a meal with them. Nada had it all worked out. We would go together to her place from work. When I was ready to return to the hotel, she would bring me back. I felt at ease with her and was looking forward to going there and building a real friendship.

One day I agreed to go with her after work for lunch. When we got there her boyfriend, John, was in the kitchen preparing the meal. He smiled at me while we shook hands. Because he didn't speak our language, Nada served as interpreter.

'Tell her how pleased I am to meet her and how much I'm looking forward to our chat over lunch,' he instructed Nada to tell me. He was soft-spoken, polite and pleasant.

I thought, *he's such a nice person.* I told Nada, 'You're very lucky to have such a nice boyfriend.'

She smiled and translated for John. He smiled and nodded his approval.

He asked me a series of questions (through Nada), 'Why did you come over to London? How long do you intend to stay in England? Do you have plans to do anything more glamorous than housekeeping?'

I answered them, as one does, during casual conversation. Then John told Nada to communicate something to me that took me by surprise.

'Nada, tell your friend that she's beautiful and sexy. 'His smile turned from friendly to disturbing.

I was embarrassed by his remark. This was inappropriate to say to someone he had just met, especially as he was asking his girlfriend to translate.

Shifting in my chair and trying to make myself as small as possible, I asked Nada, 'Did I understand that correctly? Did John just say something about my appearance?' My voice was almost a whisper by the time I finished asking her.

She waved her hand across her face as if shooing away a pest, shooing away my concerns. 'Yes, but don't worry. He's like that. He likes to flirt. He doesn't mean anything serious by it.'

If Nada was trying to reassure me, it didn't work. I became fidgety, began to look around, and ask about the time.

John gave Nada a look that said, *do something!*

So, Nada tried to ease my mind by saying, 'John is a nice person, but at times he can be unpredictable. You don't know what he'll say or do next. He's just funny that way.'

Thinking back on it now, she was probably giving me a warning, but I didn't understand. I felt because she was my friend and from my own country, she would look after me and make sure that I was safe.

John was pleasant during the lunch, but I got more nervous and worried as the conversation took this strange turn. I didn't like either of their comments, and I began wondering exactly what she had said to him about me, and what he would say or do next.

When they began speaking only English, I got panicky. They were in control of this situation. I was in their flat, and no one knew I was there. God was the only one that could help me to get out of there safely.

As John kept talking to Nada, they were staring at me. I desperately wanted to know what they were saying. Then he approached me, getting too close and putting his hands on my back, arms, and face. He was behaving as if I, not Nada, was his girlfriend. I was petrified and realised there was no escape for me. John had moved well beyond flirting.

Little did I know that the two of them planned this whole thing. Shortly after we finished lunch, Nada said to me in Serbian, 'I'm going with the dog to buy something from the shop across the road. You stay here with John, and

I'll be back in a minute. 'Her voice had lost its friendliness; it had a hard edge to it.

As she stood up to leave, I stood up too. 'I'm coming with you,' I said, my quivering voice revealing my anxiety. When I tried to follow her, she slammed the front door and disappeared.

John pushed the door further to make sure it was closed properly. He took hold of my left hand to pull me in, to keep me behind the closed doors. Nada, my supposed friend, was gone and didn't get back for a little over an hour.

That hour was the longest hour of my life thus far.

That animal grabbed me and started kissing me. He touched me all over and kept talking words I couldn't understand. His demeanour transformed from a nice, pleasant guy to an overwrought, un controlled lunatic. When I looked at his face, it was the face of evil. His eyes were rolling, and he was red-faced.

I was terrified. Not knowing what he had planned for me, I doubted I would get out of that flat alive.

The next thing I knew, he was showing me that I should go upstairs with him. I wondered what he could do to me up there that he couldn't do down where we were?

When I resisted, he slapped me across the face and showed me with his hands that if I screamed, he would slash my throat. He pulled me by my long dark hair with one hand and pointed with the other hand to go upstairs. He looked enraged. Intimidating. Menacing.

I didn't dare disobey him.

I frantically hoped that Nada would walk in at any moment to stop him, but there was no sign of her. As time passed, I realised that the two of them must have planned this. I trusted her, but she'd betrayed me by offering me to her boyfriend and then leaving the house so he could satisfy his perverted needs.

Upstairs, he led me to their bathroom. When I saw the bath filled with water and bath foam in it, I froze.

'Take your clothes off. All of them. And get in. 'John spoke like a military officer: clipped, emotionless, bullying.

I stood for a moment, shaking as if the room was frigid.

'Now!' he shouted, as he mimed undressing.

I jumped.

He laughed a joyless, ominous laugh.

I had no choice. I nodded and began taking my clothes off. My fingers fumbled due to nerves. I hoped that he wouldn't get angrier. I decided that complying with his request might be my only chance to survive this nightmare I naively wandered into.

I was right.

That animal did not rape me but sexually assaulted me. When he had enough of his pleasure, I was allowed to dress and go downstairs.

When Nada finally returned, she didn't say a word to either of us. She just kept staring at me with hatred in her eyes.

I gathered my things to leave as quickly as possible. Before I left, John put one hand over his mouth and one on my shoulder. He glared at me. What I understood from his gesture was: *if you tell anyone what happened, I will hunt you down and kill you.*

Nada and John glanced at each other, and then I was chucked out. John pushed me out of the front door and onto the street. Like a bag of garbage.

I cried all the way back to the hotel, shaking as if my body was the epicentre of a massive earthquake. I was traumatised. I was in shock. Filled with shame, I blamed myself for what happened. *Maybe I gave John a signal I didn't mean to? Maybe I should have resisted? If I understood English, maybe I could have prevented this. Maybe this is what city-dwellers do, and I over-reacted? Maybe, maybe, maybe...*

When I got back to the hotel, I went straight to my room and cried for hours. My friends were concerned. 'Why are you crying, Dragica? What happened? Tell us. It will make you feel better. Can we get you anything?'

I was both ashamed of going to Nada's flat without really knowing her and too afraid to tell anyone the truth. Instead, I told them that I was homesick. For a long time after that incident, I had nightmares and flashbacks and kept thinking how lucky I was to get out of there alive.

The next day at work, I went to see my so-called friend, Nada, who could have cost me my life. I never liked conflict, but I needed to understand why a woman would do that to another woman.

'Nada, why did you set me up with your boyfriend?' I did my best to keep my voice level.

She looked everywhere but at me. 'We should get back to work. 'Her voice sounded strained.

'What you two did was terrible. I'm going report the matter to our boss, and you know how much Bridget dislikes troublemakers. 'I lifted my chin in an attempt to be brave.

Nada's eyes widened. She stepped closer to me and, in the harshest whisper I've ever heard, said, 'I don't want to talk about it. I will only give you a message from John in case you didn't understand him. If you report us, he will look for you and kill you! Do you understand now?'

I believed the man was crazy enough to carry out his threat if I reported the assault to our boss or the police. I was frightened to leave my hotel accommodation for weeks, and I put pressure on my friend, Nina, to find us another job so we could leave the hotel. I wanted to leave for two reasons: I could 'disappear' from the man who had threatened to kill me, and I didn't have to see that traitor's (Nada's) face ever again.

As close as I was with Nina, I didn't tell her about the assault or why I wanted to leave my present job. I was embarrassed and blamed myself for trusting this female colleague and putting myself in that potentially fatal situation. I also believed that Nina would go against my wishes by reporting the incident to the police on my behalf.

In retrospect, I should have reported them to the authorities just to stop those two evil characters from abusing, torturing or harming other young women. I was just too afraid of those two people to do the right thing.

I never saw John again after that horrid day. Nada remained working in the same hotel for two years. My friend, Nina, and I moved on to work at another hotel.

When I heard the news that Holly Wells and Jessica Chapman were killed by Ian Huntley (in 2006), I was sick to my stomach for weeks and couldn't sleep properly for months. I pictured myself in those poor girls' places. When he revealed the chilling details of the girls' final moments, chills ran up and down my spine. I had an inkling of the horror they must have felt knowing they were trapped and helpless. My anger at myself for not reporting Nada and John resurfaced. Now my shame and embarrassment were because I was too much of a coward to turn them in, not because I had somehow caused my own sexual and emotional abuse.

You might ask why I chose to write openly about this now, after all this time. The answer is simple. Given recent publicity around sexual predators, I felt that it was time for me to speak up and share my experience in the hopes that others might learn from it.

While it is always my responsibility to do the right thing at all times, I still believe that God had a hand in protecting me (and still does). I thank God for looking after me when I most need him. I will always need God as I believe He is my guidance and my shadow, always behind me, protecting me from any evil

But He has a way of making me learn lessons the hard way.

Life is a Gamble

Chapter 10

Moving on to a Safe Place

Nina spoke a little English. In the latter part of 1971, she managed to get us both a job at another hotel in central London. Working there was a very daunting experience for me. That hotel was much larger, grander and fancier than the first hotel; it even had its very own theatre. I thought it was a beautiful hotel. Part of me felt fortunate to get a job in such a lovely hotel; part of me was overwhelmed with anxiety, as I kept thinking about my experience at the first hotel with the head housekeeper, Bridget. She had shaken my confidence. Was I competent enough to work in such a lush establishment?

I worked during the day, five days a week from 7am until 3 pm. One night out of those five days I was assigned to work in the evening from 5 pm to 10 pm. My job on that night was to tidy up ten bedrooms/suites and bathrooms, turn the bed sheets down for the guests and put one *After Eight* chocolate on each pillow. All of this needed to be done while the guests were out for dinner or at the theatre. Putting chocolate on the pillows was not such a good idea as very often guests would not see the chocolate or forget it was there. The next morning, some of them would complain about having melted chocolate in their hair. I thought that was funny.

As I was a new member of staff and not familiar with the large hotel, and because there were very few chambermaids on the floor at night, I hardly saw anyone. It was quite spooky. Once I was in a room, Iwas on my own. There were hotel security guards who walked round the floors once every hour – one man would do one round, then another would take a turn the next hour. They would occupy the rest of their time at the reception desk or in their office. I only ever heard them for a moment or two, so the security they provided me felt rather inadequate.

One night after I finished all the rooms, I had one remaining large apartment to tidy up. When I finished with that large apartment (by the name Maharaja), I couldn't find my way out because the apartment was so large with luxury rooms, dining rooms, lounge areas and bathrooms. Every time I opened a door, it was another cupboard or another room. I was in tears worried that I wouldn't be able to find the exit door, and the guest would return to find me wandering round in their suite. Not being able to speak

English, how would I explain that I got lost in their massive apartment? Then I remembered the number for calling the Duty Housekeeper. I called the office in a panic, whimpering, 'Maharaja, Maharaja, please, please.'

The housekeeper must have thought that I'd had some kind of accident. 'It's okay. I'm coming!' She was so worried that she didn't wait for the lift. Instead, she ran up the stairs all the way to the fifth floor. She searched the apartment and found me there crying and shaking. Confused about what had happened to upset me so, she hurried me out and found one of my Yugoslav colleagues to translate my tale for her.

The Duty Housekeeper took me off the evening shifts. That was fine with me until the following day. I was summoned to the office of the Head Housekeeper.

She sat at her desk with her fingers laced together, elbows spread, back flag-pole straight, and face as stern as a prison warden. Through a translator, she told me, 'You, young lady, are stupid! The only way I will let you work here is if you are given ten rooms somewhere in a corner where you will not get lost. You can stay and clean rooms for rest of your life. That seems all you are good and fit for. Understand?'

The translator looked past me as she communicated this harsh message.

I looked down and simply nodded my acknowledgement.

'Fine. Dismissed!'

The Head Housekeeper was in her 70s and extremely strict with everyone. I noticed that the cleaning staff all seemed afraid of her. I thought of Bridget at my first job and said to myself as I retreated from my chastisement, *here we go again. Story of my life.* But another thought also entered my head: *One day I will surprise you all. You can stand in front of me and stop me from doing things, but no one can prevent me from my destiny. One day I will be a manager. A kind, efficient manager. What I need to do is learn English. Then I will be okay.*

There was a second unpleasant incident. Nina and I shared the same room in the hotel. Nina hated to get out of bed in the morning and was often late for work. One morning, I was getting ready to start my 7am shift and kept calling to her to get up, but she wasn't having it. She asked me to tell the office that she was too ill to come to work. Being her friend, I did as she requested.

She surprised me and changed her mind. She went to work on her own floor fifteen minutes late. Approximately one hour later, the Deputy Head Housekeeper came to my floor and stormed into the room pointing her finger at me and said, 'Come with me, Miss Kuzmanovic.'

I started to tremble in front of her. I just knew something was terribly wrong, but never guessed it had anything to do with Nina.

When we arrived in the office, Nina was there.

The Deputy Head Housekeeper asked me, 'Why did you lie about this girl?'

'Nina is my –'

The interpreter, Miss Shield, stopped me, saying, 'She's not interested in your excuses. 'She quickly glanced at me with a sympathetic look before she translated the rest. 'Never. I mean never lie to any administrator, staff member or guest here again, or you will be immediately let go.'

I understood her anger. But if only she had known the real reason I lied, maybe she wouldn't have been so upset with me. I'm sure loyalty meant something to her.

I thought that if I tried harder, I wouldn't get in so much trouble. Most of the time my problems were due to the language barrier. After one year in that hotel, Nina, my friend, translator and English tutor, decided to leave the country to go back home for good. I'd learned enough English to make myself understood at work. I started to be more independent outside of work, too. I made a promise to myself to do my best so that one day I'd become a manager myself. And not just any manager. I would never treat my staff the way I'd been treated so far.

I was not stupid and was not ashamed to clean hotel rooms. It would only be a matter of time before I learned enough English to be able to move on and get a better job, which I did.

All through my life, however badly my employers or people, in general, treated me, I would be upset for a short time but would quickly bounce back. My attitude became that their anger, disappointment, frustration, or other negative view was more about them than it was about me. I still feel this today and always will. I've learned to love the jobs I did and to believe in myself. My life was about having dreams and not giving up on them. Staying positive was the only way forward.

And that's the direction I went.

Chapter 11

Stepping Up the Ladder

A year later, I had the chance to work for another hotel in London and left my job for hopefully a better opportunity. I began there as a floor housekeeper. In less than two years after my arrival in England, I was checking rooms for cleanliness instead of cleaning them. My determination to improve myself was paying off (at least career-wise), and I was quite pleased. Before the hotel was opened, I attended various courses to learn about improving customer service, developing and maintaining cleaning standards, fostering successful management practices and acquiring effective organisational skills. *Great,* I thought, *now I'm beginning to be happier at last.* At this job, the Head Housekeeper, Millie, was my perfect role model. She was caring and very protective towards her staff. I learned so much from her.

My English was still rather poor, but she had the patience of a saint. She couldn't do enough for all of her staff. I had a great deal of respect for Millie. There was nothing (within reason) that I wouldn't have done for her.

111

That woman was definitely a team player and knew how to get maximum efficiency and quality out of her staff. I was able to learn from her management style and have used it in my entire career. Her (and my) approach to management was simple: if you work with your staff and treat them with respect, they will work with you; if you don't, you will get nowhere. By threatening or humiliating others, your staff will fear you, and you have failed as a leader. I've found that this works in all facets of life.

On my first day of training, we were given a name board and letters to put our names on. Then, we were asked to introduce ourselves. My full Christian name is Dragica Kuzmanovic. There were too many letters for my name to fit on the board in front of me. A tutor helped me to shrink my first name from Dragica to Dee. I liked my new English name; it was easier for everyone to pronounce, and it sounded cheerful. I remain Dee to everyone today.

During the training, I found it difficult to write answers in English. My tutor was helpful and suggested I write in Serbian then tell her the answers. I did. It worked.

One day, I came out with, 'If I were English, I would be the best.'

My colleagues who were in that course with me roared with laughter.

The tutor just smiled at me and asked, 'What exactly do you mean, Miss Dee?'

'If I could write and explain things better in English, I would be the best in the class.'

'Oh. 'My tutor didn't know how to respond to me.

In retrospect, I know that was an arrogant thing to say – or even think. My colleagues probably thought, *what a bloody cheek! Who does she think she is?* And I wouldn't blame them one bit!

After two weeks of training, the hotel was officially opened, and I happily began my job a supervisor rather than a cleaner. I worked very hard and closely with my staff, constantly training and helping them to provide good cleaning standards for guests and the housekeeping manager. I wanted my staff to be proud of their achievements as I took great pride in my new position.

In that department, there were six Floor Housekeepers like myself, a Deputy Head Housekeeper and a Head Housekeeper. Whenever help was needed by anyone, whether in or out of my department, I was always the first one to volunteer. I got on quite well with everyone at that hotel. This was the best job I'd had so far in my career.

The job was made even sweeter because of my relationship with Millie. Although she was my superior who I deeply respected and tried to emulate, we also came to have a bond beyond our professional one. I felt for the first time since leaving home that I had someone I could talk to, rely upon, turn to for advice – a second mum. Millie always respected and appreciated what I had to say and how I was doing my job.

Life was going along smoothly for me. Finally! I worked in this new and lovely hotel for a year with people I respected and enjoyed. My English was improving all the time, and I made some nice friends that I could trust. I was relishing every moment of this life I had built for myself.

After one year, all of this changed. At one of our regular housekeeping meetings with Millie, she informed us that a Head Housekeeper from the same company, who was responsible for a small hotel near Gatwick airport, had left the job. The hotel manager was looking to replace her with someone from within the company as soon as possible. The decision about who would be promoted or transferred to that top management position in housekeeping in that hotel would be made by the following week. I was still struggling with the English language, especially written communication, so I was confident that one of my dear colleagues would be leaving. I wondered who?

To my shock and surprise, a few days later I was invited to the General Manager's office with my Head Housekeeper, Millie. Flashbacks of being brought into the boss's office to be chided for a perceived wrongdoing haunted me. But I couldn't think of anything that I had done to deserve a reprimand. Still, I was tense as I entered his office.

The General manager was standing behind his desk, which wasn't very tidy. He greeted me with a small smile and a handshake.

Millie was already there, standing in front of one of two chairs in front of his desk. Her smile was warmer than his, but she had a look in her eyes that signalled uncertainty or regret.

The General Manager motioned for us to sit.

We did. So did he. Then he nodded at Millie.

She said, 'Dee, congratulations! You've been selected as the new Head Housekeeper for a small hotel in South London.'

I wasn't sure I had heard her correctly. 'Pardon?'

'It's true. We believe you are the best person for the job. 'She nodded as she spoke as if willing me to agree.

'But…but, why me? I'm happy *here!* And I still need to improve my English…' I looked at the General Manager, but he was reading some papers. Millie was clearly in charge. She picked me for the job. She must have had faith in my managerial skills. I needed to have faith in myself, too. But that was difficult to summon. I was more or less okay with speaking basic English, but my written skills were abysmal. My telephone communications were even worse. I started to cry. With tears rolling down my face, I said, 'What about the other housekeepers? Any of them are much more qualified for the job than I am. At least they know the language.'

The General Manager and Millie looked at each other and smiled. This time he spoke. 'We know who we have here, but we also know who can do the best job, and that will be you, Miss Dee.'

Before I had a chance to say anything, Millie added, 'We are helping you, Dee, and this job will be a nice promotion for you.'

There's a well-known English proverb that says, 'Don't look a gift horse in the mouth. 'I knew I shouldn't have questioned the judgment or intentions of my superiors, but I didn't want this 'gift horse. 'Indeed, I felt as if this 'gift horse' was kicking me in the mouth, and I didn't like it one bit! But I didn't have much of a choice.

At that meeting, I was told to start packing my belongings because things were going to happen fast. The following Monday, I loaded my belongings in to a car and was taken to my new job. I was so upset that for most of the journey I hardly spoke to the driver. I felt that I left behind much-loved family and kept asking myself, *how can I get a job without an interview or, at the very least, meeting the General Manager? What if I don't like the manager or the hotel?* I suppose the thing that bothered me the most was that I wasn't given a choice. I was happy at that hotel with Millie, and I thought, *here we go again.*

Did Millie want me to leave or was she truly trying to help me in my career? I had to admit that I had grown comfortable in my job. But what's wrong with that? I don't know, but I had to keep moving forward with a positive attitude. This was, after all, a promotion.

Although the hotel was small with 70 bedrooms, I was petrified to go to an unknown location. I didn't know anyone there including my boss, the General Manager. Little did I know that he was another harsh, authoritarian manager like Bridget from my first hotel job.

When I arrived, I expected to meet an Englishman for a boss. But I was surprised. The General Manager was from India, and his name was Chan. He was very dark. All I notice were his white teeth. Before coming to the UK, I had never seen a black person. In the 1970s, there weren't that many black people in England, either. I'd never worked anywhere with black people before. For me, interacting with someone from another race wasn't a negative experience; it was a new experience. One more change to become accustomed to.

When I saw Chan for the first time, I just froze. I mumbled to the driver, 'Please take me back with you. I beg you. I don't want to stay here. 'Tears started streaming down my face. When it was clear that I couldn't stay in the car all day, I got out. One might have thought I was a grieving widow being dropped off at the funeral of my beloved late husband, handkerchief in hand, dabbing my runny nose and teary eyes.

'What's the matter with you? You *are* my new Head Housekeeper, correct?' His manner was no-nonsense, and his voice was stern. He stared into my red, weepy eyes.

I did my best to compose myself and answered, 'I am sorry, Sir. I...I simply was not prepared for this new job. It's all very...what's the word...over whelming. 'I wiped run-away tears that cascaded down the sides of my cheeks.

My new manager narrowed his eyes and said abruptly, 'Crying means nothing to me. You are here to do the job, Dee. Pull yourself together and do it.'

Oh, my God! What am I getting myself into? I thought.

After a couple of hours, Chan left to go back to London. It looked as if my problems were beginning all over again with this man. I was right.

I was a 23-year-old department head with no experience in upper management and limited English language skills in a hotel new to me. I thought, *it's happening again. I will have as hard a time with my new General Manager as I had with Bridget at the first hotel.* Again, I was right. What I didn't know at the time was that my experiences with Chan and the small hotel marked the beginning of my future successful career. Both the General Manager and Millie had told me this was my big opportunity during that difficult meeting. It would take some time before I appreciated what they did for me, though.

The hotel was bustling both day and night. Being near the airport, it had two to three occupancies daily for the same room. I could not understand why, after two hours – even after one hour –some rooms had to be cleaned again. I quickly learned that the unusually fast turnover had to do with the airport. The cabin crew would come and go at all hours of the day and night, sometimes only sleeping for one or two hours before catching another flight. That room had to be re-cleaned for the next arrival. The system was initially confusing, but I soon got used to it.

I started work at 5:30am to help the chambermaids start serving a continental breakfast at 6am and then start cleaning rooms at 7am to prepare for new guests. Because of the nature of the occupancy, I would often still be working by 10 or even 11 pm. Those were long, hard days.

On top of the workload, Chan was a demanding boss. He often asked for 'special' tasks (like errands) to be done, which added to everyone's workflow. Since making sure rooms were ready for new guests was my priority, his 'special' requests sometimes went undone. That always made him angry.

His fingers would ball up into fists, and he would pace when I had to tell him we weren't able to complete a job he had requested. 'Why not, Dee? It was not a difficult job. 'He often had to work to keep from screeching.

I purposefully would take deep breaths to calm myself before I answered. 'Sir, my staff works very hard to make sure all the rooms are spotless for your guests so that they can sleep in comfort, no matter what time they arrive. We simply did not have time today.'

He then would give me his tight-lipped, I'm-the-boss lecture. 'Dee, I want you to remember one thing from now on and keep remembering it for the rest of your career. When I ask you to do something, I expect you to do it. I will check that my request is carried out, and I am not interested who did it as long as it is done. Listen to me Dee and remember. If you don't mean to check what you have asked your staff to do, then don't bother asking them in the first place. But when you do ask them, make sure you check that is done. I hope you will remember this. 'He would then turn on his heel to leave my office in a dramatic fashion.

'Yes, sir!' I whispered after he closed my door.

On one occasion, he called me into his office to complain about kitchen and cleaning staff misusing and soiling towels and linens that were provided by a laundry company. Soot from ovens, shoe polish, or cigarette ash ruined the fabric. Thus, the hotel had to pay to replace the damaged items *and* pay for laundering services. Chan was not happy.

Rather than inform me of the problem and let me talk to my staff, he felt I needed to be educated about the laundry business. Chan called me to his office. He called the laundry manager and said, 'I have a very good housekeeper, but she is foreign and doesn't speak much English. Can I send her round to you so you can explain to her and show her how the linen is washed and what happens if the linen is damaged by the customer?'

After my visit to the laundry company, I was much more informed about the laundry business, which is never a bad thing. Chan gave me strict instructions concerning any lost or damaged linen: lie to the laundry service. Tell them that I had received less linen than I'd sent out to the laundry company for washing.

Following this direct order from my supervisor felt wrong. My parents taught me to be honest and lying for Nina that one time had nearly gotten me sacked. But I was afraid to cross Chan, so I did the only thing I could think of to do: stock more linen than I started with and kept it that way while working for him. Also, I emphasised to my staff the importance of not using towels or linens as cleaning cloths.

Chan exploited and bullied me in many ways – subtle and obvious – from the first day I started working at the hotel. I was getting tired and felt unwell, often suffering from stress and exhaustion. After nine or ten months of his harassment, I was ready to confront him and tell him how I felt.

Before I spoke to Chan, I was called into his office by his secretary.

He was oddly calm when he told me, 'I will be leaving at the end of the month to manage another hotel in Borehamwood Herts. They are owned by the same company. 'He waited for my reaction.

I wanted to say, *that's such good news! Thank God, I won't be working for you anymore! I'll never have to see you again. You have just made my day!* Instead, I said, 'Congratulations, Sir.'

My joy was short-lived.

He flashed those white teeth at me. 'Dee, you are doing a good job here, but I want you to come with me. When I leave here, I will be in touch.'

I was so afraid of him that I replied, 'Okay, we'll see.'

'Nothing to see,' he said. 'You *will* be coming to join me. Do you hear me?'

'Yes, Sir,' I said. I thought, *not in a million years!*

I figured that once he was gone, he would never see me again. He would find someone new to bully.

The following week, my new manager was shown round and introduced to all the staff at the hotel by Chan while he was working his notice. The new manager was lovely. He had a young family –a wife and baby girl.

When he met me, he said, 'Dee, I have had a good report about you from Chan. I want to keep you here and look after you. I understand that you are living in one room at the moment. When Chan leaves, I will move you to a one-bedroom apartment here in the hotel. It will be nice if you would help us with babysitting if and when we need you.'

'That would be lovely. Thank you!'

I was delighted with what he offered me. And he presented it as a proposal, not a command.

I would have moved into my new flat, content to stay as Head Housekeeper of this small, busy hotel, but one month later I received a phone call from Chan's secretary. All she said was, 'Dee, Chan wants to speak to you.'

She didn't say, 'Chan *would like* to speak *with* you. '*Same old bully,* I thought. *Why won't he leave me alone?* I didn't have to take his call, but I did. I was still afraid of him and what he might do (tell the new manager some lie about me?). When I heard his voice, my heart pounded. My legs shook like jelly on the plate of a running toddler.

He said, 'Dee, I want you to come and work for me. I need you at this hotel. It is very dirty, and you and I need to put it right.'

I summoned my courage and said, 'I'm sorry, Sir. I'm happy where I am. And what I would tell my new manager? He would be very upset if I left. 'I closed my eyes, waiting for his response.

'I don't care. Tell him you are going back to Yugoslavia, China or whatever, but I want you here by the end of the next week. Friday. Do you hear me?'

I answered quietly, 'Yes, Sir. 'I was genuine frightened of this man. He was a crazy man who always shouted at his staff. Stress and guilt plagued me when I lied to my new manager about going back to my native country. I gave him one week's notice and left in September 1973.

Chan had a frightening hold on me. He was very strict and unreasonable. I was not strong enough to stand up for myself and didn't have anyone to protect me. I felt like a small fish in the big sea. Chan was always shouting at everyone (apart from the guests), and he got away with it for years because everyone was too afraid to complain. That kind of behaviour in today's work environments would never be tolerated.

However, I learned valuable lessons about how to be a good manager from this dreadful manager. One lesson was how to check rooms and make sure that they were cleaned spotlessly at all times. Another was how to look after linen by making sure that staff did not use it as cleaning rags. I also learned from Chan that when I ask my staff to do something, I should make sure I check that is done.

Perhaps the most valuable lesson I learned from my time at my most recent former job was not to say 'no' to new opportunities even if they scared me. Just when I settled into a comfortable situation, something (or someone) disrupted it. Rather than lamenting the loss, I was slowly learning to accept the challenge. And, oh, there would be many more challenges to come.

Life is a Gamble

Chapter 12

Not Getting Out of It

Chan arranged for a car to pick me up from my now former job and take me to my new accommodation that was rented by the owners of the new hotel at which I would be working. With Chan. Again.

I shared the house with three other young women: Jean, Karen and Antonia, who welcomed me and were supportive. The following Monday, I reported for work. After a tour of the hotel with the manager, I realised that I had made a big mistake leaving my previous hotel that was new and spotlessly clean.

Oh dear, what have I landed myself in to? I thought at the time. The hotel was very old, neglected and filthy. Each bedroom had a proper mini-red phone box like the ones on the street. It's hard to believe that today, but that was how it was in the 1970s. The hotel was mainly used by actors and actresses who were filming at Elstree Studios.

On the first day in that hotel, I had a meeting with my staff, I informed them of what I expected from them and explained how my expectations would be met. 'I will be starting mandatory training about health and safety and how to clean rooms properly. Also, how to make the beds with hospital corners.'

My staff looked at each other, shifted in their seats, and seemed uncomfortable. But no one objected. Yet.

'Don't worry. I'll work with you to achieve good cleaning standards for the guests who are paying to stay here. 'I smiled at them. 'Our guests are entitled to have the best service and comfort, not just in their rooms but all round the hotel. 'I thought I had given a professional, inspiring pep talk to my new staff.

These chambermaids, however, we reused to doing things their own way for a long time. By the looks of it, 'their own way' was to do as little cleaning as possible round the hotel. One of my new staff told me, 'Excuse me, Ma'am. We've been here for years and know how to clean. We don't need any training. 'She crossed her arms over her chest. Most of them nodded and did the same.

I could see they did not want to change their ways. Taking a deep breath, I used my management skills and told them, 'I'm not criticising you for what you have done up till now. I'm sure you've done everything your former Head Housekeeper asked of you. But now that I'm here, things must change because they need to be done my way. The only way this partnership will be successful is if we all work as a team. Together we can achieve good cleaning standards, and everyone will benefit. I promise.'

I was getting pressure from the manager to get the hotel cleaned up as soon as possible. At the same time, I was getting grief from the staff who didn't want to be trained for the job they were getting paid for. They had created a wall between them and me that was difficult to breach, but I had to convince them how important the training was for them. Some of them were as hard as granite to crack, but it was up to me to be patient and work with them to achieve my goal.

Since the professional manger approach was failing, I decided to try something more personal. At another staff meeting, I explained to them why I was brought in by Chan. Maybe my story would soften them. 'You've probably experienced this too, but I was treated quite unkindly by some of my superiors in the past.'

Most nodded or muttered agreement.

'A lot of my problems had to do with me not being able to express myself because I didn't speak English at all. They thought I was stupid! That made me so angry.'

I heard several, 'Yes, me, too!' comments among my audience.

'It's so unfair. Because I came from where you are, I know how hard your job is. It's not just the demands of the job; it's all the other indignities that come with it.'

A chorus of women said, 'Yes!'

'Yes! Well, I am here to stay with you, work with you and support you. I will always speak to and treat my staff and colleagues as I would like to be treated and spoken to, *never* how I was treated and spoken to in the past by my insensitive superiors.'

Whether they felt sorry for me or felt as if I was truly one of them, I won their hearts. The atmosphere in the room changed from resentment to openness; it was palpable.

I smiled. 'Do you have any questions for me or should we get on with the training?'

The one who had spoken up the first time was the one to speak again. 'We're sorry about any misunderstanding, right?' She looked round at her colleagues. They all nodded their agreement. 'And we would like to go through your training.'

I felt that my honesty and firmness about my aim had worked. When I finished with the training session, I thanked them and told them, 'Well done! We can and will work together to make this hotel one of the best in the area.'

And we did. I was very proud of them.

I am a great believer in learning to work *with* my staff, not against them. I don't like power games. I've always tried to remember what I learned from Nina, one of my previous line managers. She used to say, 'Be firm, be fair, then be friendly. And never the other way round. Otherwise, it won't work. 'She was right. Her advice worked for me for the next 43 years of my career. What also helped me through my entire working carrier was for me to give my staff respect first. I always spoke to them the way I would have liked to be spoken to, not the other way round; it worked every time.

From then on, I didn't look back and magic happened. I continued training my staff and worked with them diligently by helping them to clean rooms and make beds. Within a short time, the entire hotel was beautifully clean. My staff kept proper cleaning standards at all times. Guests, staff and visitors began to notice the improved cleanliness and orderliness of the hotel. I felt the best reward we could all get was to have both happy staff and happy guests.

Chan, however, never seemed satisfied. Whenever we had a meeting, he didn't ask how I was doing. Instead, he would always say to me, 'Dee, it is not too bad. but you need to push your staff to work harder.'

'Yes, Sir. 'I always humbly replied while holding back the urge to defend my conscientious, meticulous staff and tell him how discouraged and inept he made me feel.

Sometimes I overheard guests compliment the housekeeping services or someone from head office would ask him, 'What is your housekeeper like?'

His response was always the same thing, 'I wouldn't replace my Yugoslavian housekeeper for three West-End housekeepers. She is brilliant. The best.'

I would hear this from others, too, but he never told me directly. it hurts when all you hear is criticism from your boss. Never a compliment. Never a word of encouragement. I praised my staff, and they loved it. It's a simple matter of treating people as valued members of a team. I always marvelled at how many managers didn't understand this.

Not only did I praise my staff individually and in staff meetings, I told anyone inside and outside the hotel how brilliant my staff were and how blessed I was to have them.

Once my staff understood that I was the kind of manager who treated them with respect and kindness, they were supportive towards me. I shared positive feedback with the group. When we received negative feedback about any staff member, I made it about having to fix a policy (not about them). We would then collectively put it right as soon as possible and turn the negative feedback into a positive lesson. This created loyalty in my staff, and the hotel benefited from the resulting quality improvements.

Many people do not see value in housekeeping as a career. I see it as an important, even key, element in the hospitality business. It is demanding work that often gets noticed only when it's not done properly. I took pride in making sure the job was done correctly and that my staff felt dignified doing it. There are no small jobs in this world, only small minds. Having tried to instil this ethic in my staff over the years was quite important to me.

Unfortunately, there were many people in my life (past and those yet to come) who were small-minded and tried to uproot my fledgling sense of myself as a confident, competent woman.

Life is a Gamble

Chapter 13

Meeting My Mystery Man

After I had been working at the hotel for three months, I felt fairly comfortable with my staff and the routines I created. On Christmas day of that year (1973), we worked from 9am to 5pm.

At the end of the day, my colleague, Antonia, came to my office and said, 'Dee, Karen and Jean want us to go home with them in the taxi.'

'What? I thought we would just walk and save ourselves some money.'

Antonia seemed impatient. 'You know we are having a party at our house tonight, right? We need to go with them to help with preparations. A taxi will get us there quicker.'

I agreed to go with them.

When we got on our road, the taxi driver stopped at number 9instead of 37, where we all lived. Karen and Jean said, 'Come on, let's go!'

'Antonia,' I whispered, 'where are we going?'

She smiled. 'To the driver's boss' house for a quick drink.

I frowned and shook my head.

Antonia patted my hand and winked at me. 'Don't worry,' she said, 'they're friendly with Karen and Jean. It'll be fun!'

I did worry, though. Images of my nasty experience shortly after I arrived in the UK with those two predators, Nada and John, flashed in my head like ambulance emergency lights. One innocent misjudgement had nearly cost me my life and still provoked a great deal of fear. So, this situation naturally made me a bit nervous; even though there were four of us girls together.

All three of them put pressure on me and said basically the same thing, 'Please, come on! What's the matter with you? No one is going to eat you up.'

How can you be so sure? How well do you know anyone? That's what I wanted to ask them, but their collective giddy-with-delight eyes persuaded me to trust them. At least I wouldn't be alone, or so I hoped.

When we got in the house, the taxi driver offered us all drinks. The house looked as though a woman living there; it was tidy and nicely decorated. Something about how well the place was kept-up made me relax a bit.

Within five minutes, a short, chubby, bald gentleman walked into the room with a bowl of homemade salad in his hands. He said, 'Hello! Good to see you Karen and Jean! And who do you have with you? I'm Mike.'

Antonia introduced herself and said, 'This is Dee. She's the Head Housekeeper at the hotel where we all work. Nice to meet you, Mike.'

As he started offering the salad to each of, telling us to help ourselves with the same spoon, he spoke to me, 'Head Housekeeper? That's impressive for one so young!'

'Thank you. 'My reply was reserved, but polite. 'How do you know Jean and Karen?

'Oh, I used to take them to and from work in my taxi. Now I'm the Regional Director for a company that handles the city' s parcel transport needs. Quite a success story. I'll have to tell you about it someday.' If he could have grown taller with each word he uttered, he would have. What he lacked in looks, he made up for in arrogance.

I had never met him before, and I thought him quite vulgar to offer the same dish and the same spoon for everyone to use. *How unhygienic*, I thought. I politely refused to take any salad that was offered to me.

Mike asked me, 'Where are you from?'

'Yugoslavia.'

'Ah, I have a friend from Yugoslavia. She's very nice. 'He winked at me.

I tried not to shudder.

We all had a couple of drinks and were ready to leave. Mike offered to take us in his car to our house.

I asked Antonia, "Why go by car? We only live up the road a bit."

Mike jumped into our conversation. "I don't like my guests to walk when I can easily drive them. Transport is my speciality, after all!" He grabbed his keys and dangled them in front of us.

Jean smiled and said, "Thanks, Mike! You're a doll!" She had made our decision for us.

As there was not enough space in the car, Jean sat on Mike's lap next to his driver in the front seat. Jean and Mike were messing about with Jean kissing Mike on the neck and other provocative behaviours. I thought, *oh, God, how could she kiss such an ugly person.* It was like watching young kids playing. *Hopefully, they're enjoying themselves,* I thought.

When they dropped us off, I just said bye and ran into the house. Later that evening, quite a few people came to our Christmas party. One of the party guests was Mike. I was dancing with a young man, and, when we finished, I went upstairs to my bedroom to get something. On the way down, Mike told me I was a beautiful girl. My heart started racing. I was a shy person, not used to such bold statements, but that's not why I reacted so intensely. His compliment immediately brought back horrible memories of being set-up by Nada with that creepy John. I quickly returned to the room where everyone was dancing so I wouldn't be alone.

Mike reached for my hand and asked me to dance. The boy that I was dancing with earlier took my hand instead. I told Mike that I was with him. Mike apologised to him. I wasn't with anyone at the time, but I only danced with that boy.

Later in the evening, Antonia told me that she was invited to a dinner date.

'That's so nice,' I said. 'Who is the lucky fellow then?'

'You probably won't believe it, but it's Mike. 'She waited for my reaction, staring into my eyes.

'What did you say?'

'Unfortunately for him, I said no.'

'Antonia, I think you made a wise choice. Even stone drunk, I wouldn't go out with him. 'We both laughed.

I didn't see or hear from Mike for the next couple of months even though he lived just down the road from me. I was neither bothered by nor interested in him, so that was fine with me.

One evening before I left work, I received a phone call from Mike. He wanted to take me out to dinner. I was so unpleasantly surprised by his phone call that when he said hello, I fell silent, hoping he would disappear off the line, and I wouldn't hear from him ever again.

He didn't give up easily. 'Can't make up your mind? Well, I'll make it up for you, Dee. I'll wait for you when you finish work tonight. How does that sound?'

I didn't give in easily. 'Thank you, but I can't.'

'Okay, but what about tomorrow or some other time?'

'I don't know, but I don't think so.'

The very next day, he was waiting for me to finish work. When I came out, he asked, 'You must be hungry. May I take you out for dinner?' He had the eager hopefulness on his face that a dog has when waiting for someone to give him a treat.

I made some silly excuse and said as firmly as I could, '*No*. But, thank you.'

Mike was so persistent that eventually I gave in and agreed for him to pick me up the next day. 'But don't come to the house. I'll come out instead. 'I was thinking about what my housemates would say if they saw me with him after what I had said in the past about him being bald, ugly and fat.

He agreed to meet me in a public place.

When I got in his car, I told Mike I would only go out with him as a friend. 'That means if you try to make any kind of move on me, I won't go out with you ever again. 'I know that this was a stern, hostile way to begin a 'date,' but my safety was my priority.

I must say he was a perfect gentleman. So, I agreed to continue seeing him. When we got more comfortable with each other, Mike started telling me little bits of his life story. He was married before and had a daughter who was a few months old when we met. His wife had left with his six-weeks-old baby at the beginning of September 1973, around the same time I moved from Crawley near Gatwick, but I didn't meet Mike until Christmas three months later.

'She left you and took your daughter away from you? That seems terribly harsh. 'I felt sorry for him, and my attitude about him softened.

'Dee, she had good reasons. She left me because of my gambling habit. I lost quite a lot of money. After losing the money, I was afraid to go home and face the music, so I ran away to Scotland. 'His head was hanging as he spoke.

I didn't know what to say, so I reached across the table and patted his hand.

We exchanged sad smiles, and he continued. 'When my father found out what happened, he went looking for me and brought me back home to my wife. When I got back, my wife's parents were in the house waiting for me. They told me they would be taking their daughter and granddaughter home with them, and that she will not be coming back to their matrimonial home.'

'You must have been devastated!'

'Yes, I was. But I also understood. You see, this wasn't the first time I'd let my gambling habit go too far and lost too much money. But I've learned my lesson now. I've given up gambling for good!'

'Oh, Mike. Good for you!' We smiled at each other again, but this time, we were both filled with joy and celebration.

I believed him. Although he told me all about his gambling at that time, I was green as grass and had no knowledge about gambling and what impact it can have on both the person who gambles and their family. It never crossed my mind that I would be his next wife and what impact his gambling would have on me.

We continued to see each other as platonic friends (as far as I was concerned) and, as a friend, I was very sympathetic and a good listener for him. Little did I know that he had fallen in love with me from the minute he saw me. Mike was serious about me the whole time. We saw each other regularly for about three months.

One evening, we were a little close to each other, and we kissed. After that kiss, I was so embarrassed and angry with myself. I felt as if I had let myself down. A romantic relationship with Mike (or anyone) was not what I wanted. I needed to focus on my career. I stood up and left his house.

I was always positive, determined and more interested in improving myself by developing a successful professional career rather than finding a husband and being dependant on him. If I stayed in Hertfordshire, I was afraid that Mike would never leave me alone, and he would somehow hold me back in my career. The only way for him to stop pestering me was for me to vanish from his life. Yes, I would be leaving a good job, but I was sure I could find another, better, opportunity. Within the next few days, I found a job that was advertised in the *Evening Standard* for the position of Head Housekeeper for a hotel in central London.

When I told Mike that I was leaving my job and moving, he was upset and wanted to know where I was going. He said he wanted to help me by taking me and my belongings to my new job. I thanked him for the offer and told him that everything had been arranged, but the truth was I didn't want him to know where I was going.

A few days later, I took a taxi and all my belongings and went to my new job to meet my predecessor, the Head Housekeeper, who was leaving the hotel that day. It was important for me to meet this person before she left as I needed to go through a departmental handover.

On my arrival at the hotel, I was greeted by the Hotel Manager. My belongings were left with the concierge until my predecessor vacated the apartment assigned to the Head Housekeeper. The apartment was on the same street, opposite the hotel. The same afternoon I was taken by my new manager to meet the Head Housekeeper in her office. The office was located in the basement, which had no carpet, amplifying every footstep when someone was walking. As we walked along this long corridor, I heard someone walking very firmly, and it sounded like a woman's stiletto shoe.

What went through my mind at that point was, *oh my God! It reminds me of Bridget's footsteps from my first job. Surely, it's not her. It can't be. This is too small a hotel for her.* Shivers ran up and down my spine.

At that point, it had been three years since I'd left that hotel, but I was right; it was Bridget. What a surprise that was! I will never forget the knock on the departing Head Housekeeper's office door. This little four-foot, six-inch person appeared in front of me and introduced herself as Bridget, the Head Housekeeper. She shook my hand and said, 'Pleased to meet you.'

Oh no! Surely not her...not Bridget, I thought. I felt panic welling up inside of me but managed to stay calm on the outside. To see this person again – in a different circumstance– was one of the biggest surprises I've experienced in my entire career. Perhaps hers, too. We both pretended that we didn't know each other.

Yes, it was Bridget from my first job in England for whom I worked as a chambermaid and of whom I was petrified. It was almost unbelievable how far I'd gone in three short years, but the fear remained as strong as if I'd never left her employ. When she knew me, I couldn't speak English at all and treated like an idiot. Now, I was replacing her as head of the housekeeping department, and all within three years. After I got over the shock of seeing her, I allowed myself to feel very proud and dignified, too. *Good on me*, I thought. *Eat your heart, Bridget. I'm not as stupid as you thought.* She was one bully who failed in breaking her target's spirit! Well, almost.

Bridget went through the handover books, telling me what I needed to know. Her Northern Irish accent was as thick as ever. I understood English but still couldn't understand most of what she was saying. But I didn't ask her to repeat herself. It was as though I was still frightened of her and kept replying 'yes, yes, yes' to everything she said just as I did when I didn't understand English. I suppose old habits and fears die hard.

After the handover, Bridget shook my hand, wished me luck and left. I moved into the same apartment she had lived in. As I was looking around, I thought that it was unusual for a hotel to provide the following for staff: pots and pans, television, iron and ironing board and other household conveniences. And they didn't. Bridget left her personal belongings for the next person, who happened to be me. *Great,* I thought, *but why didn't she take her personal things?*

The following evening, the phone rang in my apartment. I answered.

Someone said, 'Hello, is this Miss Kuzmanovic?'

I recognised her Irish accent straightaway.

'It's me, Bridget, 'she said.

My first reaction was panic. 'Could you please wait a moment?' I placed my hand over the mouthpiece and took a deep breath. Then I said slowly, cautiously, 'Yes Bridget, can I help you?'

'No. I am ringing to tell you that everything in that apartment apart from the bed, wardrobe and bed cabinet, I left for you.'

I quietly answered her, 'Thank you, Bridget. That was very nice of you.'

'You are welcome,' she said, 'but what I also wanted to say to you, Miss Kuzmanovic, is well done on your achievement. I must tell you that as much as I thought I would die tomorrow, I believed that you would get into my shoes as quickly as you have done. And one more thing I would like to say to you is that if you carry on being positive, enthusiastic, and determined as you have been up till now, you will go a long way with your career. Good luck, Miss Kuzmanovic, and goodbye.'

Bridget's praise and encouragement were unexpected but helped me a great deal. Regardless of her sour demeanour, she was one of the best Head Housekeepers in London. From then on, when I was under pressure and thought I couldn't do something, I could almost hear her voice saying, 'Yes, you can do it,' and I carried on.

I'd just gotten over the shock of meeting Bridget again but was still convinced I'd never see Mike again. I don't know how he found me, but two weeks after I left Hertfordshire, things started to happen. Yet again, this was not what I wanted to happen.

One morning, Reception called to tell me that there had been a gift delivered for me. They wanted me to come down to collect it. As I was very busy working, I told the reception staff that I would collect it at the end of my working day. At 3:30pm, I was leaving the hotel to go to my apartment opposite the hotel and forgot to collect the parcel from Reception. Before I reached the front door, I was called back and handed large bouquet of red roses. I wondered who knew I was there and who they were from?

I opened the envelope and read the card. It said:

'Thank you for being my Dragica.'

Mike.

I worried about how he found out where I had gone and what was coming next. As I came out of the hotel clutching those red roses in my arm, I looked across the road. Who did I see? Mike with his cousin. My legs became jelly. The embarrassing thing was that I was clutching the roses that he had sent. I was already out of the hotel. We had seen each other, so there was no point in me going back into the hotel.

As I got near them, Mike said, 'Hello, Dee.'

I said a clipped, 'Hello,' but kept walking toward my accommodation.

'Hey, Dee, can we come to yours for a cup of tea? I really want to talk to you.'

Still walking, I replied, 'No! You can't come. I've got nothing to say to you, and I don't want to listen to what you have to say. Just go away and leave me alone. 'I quickened my pace.

Not willing to give up easily, he kept up with me and said, 'I just want you to know that no matter what, one day I will marry you, and you will be my wife.'

Achill ran down my spine. I kept walking and thinking, *what's so hard to understand? I don't like you!* I couldn't imagine ever loving him.

I finally made it to my flat. Alone. I looked out of the window through the curtains. He stayed with his cousin outside my accommodation for a further 45 minutes before they left.

The next day, he somehow got hold of my telephone number and kept calling me after work, telling me how much he missed me and lived for the day when I would agree to meet him at least for a coffee. At that time, I didn't understand what stalking meant, but Mike's behaviour certainly fits the definition of a stalker.

I did the worst thing I could do in that type of situation: I gave in and eventually agreed to meet with him. We met in the local cafe bar. Before I gave him a chance to say anything, I told him, 'Leave me alone or I'll report you to the police.'

He said, 'I'm sorry you feel that way, but please give me at least a chance to explain. You're a kind woman, Dee. All I'm asking for is a little kindness. Please?' Mike was a manipulative person, but I wasn't aware of this at the time.

He began crying.

I didn't know what to do. I wanted him to leave me alone, but I felt it would be cruel to turn my back on such a distraught person. 'Why are you so upset? Things can't be that bad.' I said in an effort to be nice, but not too nice.

'Oh, Dee! I've lost everything because of my gambling. But I've learned my lesson for good. I'm a changed man and gambling is out of my blood for ever. The only thing that keeps me going is the hope that you and I can be together. I have never loved anyone as much as I love you. You can save me, Dee. Only you.'

I was so naïve that I started to feel sorry for him. No man had ever spoken to me like that – had ever entrusted his life to me. I convinced myself that I could save him from his gambling habits so that we could live happily ever after.

Because Mike professed such deep love for me, he seemed less unpleasant. We began to date and eventually I fell in love with him. In the meantime, my ex-manager, Chan, called me to apologise yet again for the way he treated me before I left the job and asked me to return to work for him again. The timing seemed right, so I accepted his offer. But now I had Mike to think about. I was no longer making decisions just for myself. With this job offer from Chan, I thought I could be with Mike and have a good local job. In June 1974, I moved back to Hertfordshire to my old job and lived with Mike.

I believe Mike when he kept telling me how much he loved me and that he would do everything in his power to make me happy. Yes, he did love me, but my happiness was like a yoyo – up and down –for the duration of our relationship. I'm sure to this day that he meant what he said at the time he said it.

A month later, in July 1974, he came home one evening with a big bunch of flowers and an engagement ring. He bent on one knee and asked, 'Dee, will you make me the happiest man on Earth and marry me?' Genuine hope gleamed in his eyes as he placed the bouquet on my lap.

I pushed the flowers to the floor and started to cry.

Mike's face twisted in bewilderment. His voice was gentle when he asked, 'Dee, what's wrong? Don't you want to marry me?'

I stared at my empty lap when I replied, 'Yes, I want to marry you, but I'm worried about my deformed foot. You might regret marrying me one day.'

He ran his hands over his face and scalp, sighing. Then he took my hands in his. 'I love *you*. I'm marrying you, not your foot. Your bad foot is part of you. I told you about my mother's accident and that she lost part of her leg when she was eleven-years-old when a bus hit her. But my father loved her. He was always supportive and protective towards her. That's how I'll be with you. I love you. *Please* marry me.'

How lovely it was to hear this. He said all the right things in just the right ways. I felt lucky to marry someone who really loved me and would do anything for me. I accepted his proposal. Gladly.

***

Little did I know at the time that compulsive gamblers don't simply stop because they say they want to. During our engagement, we stayed in Mike's matrimonial home until his house was repossessed. We had to move into a rented accommodation in Hendon, North West London. We stayed there for a few months but could not afford the rent as it increased after a short time.

In October 1974, we moved to North Finchley, North London, and on 4 December 1974, we got married. My wedding day was supposed to be the happiest day of my life. It wasn't. My beloved family members were not with me on my special day because none of them could afford to pay for their tickets to come over from Yugoslavia, and we couldn't afford to pay for any of them. His family boycotted our wedding because they were angry with him for ruining his first marriage with a nice Jewish girl because of his gambling.

For a while, we were happy together. Three months after we got married, Mike found an advert in the Hackney Gazette for some kind promotion from the local housing authority in Hackney. They were giving one or two-bedroom council flats to people who wished to queue 24 hours to qualify. The first 100 people in the queue would get the keys the following day and be able to move in immediately.

Life is a Gamble

This was in March 1975. The weather was bitterly cold with a lot of snow on the ground. We got ready with blankets, hot drinks and sandwiches, got in the car and made our way to Hackney. When we got there, we saw a very long queue.

We thought there was no chance; we'd missed it. But when Mike counted the people in front of us, we couldn't believe our luck. We were number 98 in the queue. *How lucky we are*, I thought. We jumped up and down with joy.

Our flat was on the 4th floor. It wasn't much, but it was ours.

We were so desperate to have our own, affordable accommodation. With both of us in full-time employment (me as Head Housekeeper and Mike as Regional Director of the transportation company), we wanted to save a deposit to buy our own property and hopefully start a family. During that cold and long March night, we took turns sleeping in the car while one of us stayed in the queue.

The following day, it took the housing department staff most of the day to sort out the paperwork for the people who qualified to collect the keys. When we picked up our keys, I was over the moon, as that council flat was my first permanent accommodation in England. For the first time, I(we) didn't have to share a front door with other people. We had our own front door.

Unlike during our wedding, Mike was not as happy as I was. He told me that his parents had worked very hard and fought for years to leave the East End behind to live in a better area. 'And here I am after all my years of hard work. Back where I bloody started.'

I rubbed his back and told him, "It's not forever, Darling. If we work hard and save enough money for a deposit, then we can buy our own property and move back to North London. Then we'll be close to your parents. Won't that be grand?"

He shrugged his shoulders and grumbled something I was glad not to hear.

Over time, we managed to save £5,000. The plan was to continue saving for the deposit to purchase our first property together. One day when I was off work, the letter box rattled at mid-day. When I went to the front door, there was a single brown envelope on the floor. I opened that envelope. To my utter surprise, I was holding the building society accounts book (which recorded our savings for our eventual new property and home). It had been returned to us because the account had no money in it. Zero.

Standing at the door holding the accounts book with a £0 balance, I was immobilised with shock. I couldn't (and didn't want to) believe what I saw. Only Mike and I had access to this money. I didn't take it, so Mike did. Without telling me. Why? Slowly, it dawned on me that Mike was gambling again. He took *our* money for *our* future and gambled it away. No wonder his first wife left him with their daughter who was only six-weeks-old at the time.

When he got home from work, I confronted him about the empty building society book. He looked like a frightened rabbit cornered by a hungry fox. But I certainly didn't feel sly or superior to this man who duped me. Yes, I was angry but in the way that any person who is betrayed by someone they love and trust gets angry. My anger masked how profoundly hurt I was.

As I was demanding to know why he gambled our savings and going ballistic at him regarding the money and our future together, he was so apologetic and kept saying that he was sorry. He had made a mistake. 'I thought I could double the money so we can move out of here quicker. I love you. I can't live without you. You are my life, and if you leave me my life won't be worth living. Please, please forgive me.'

It crossed my mind to leave him, but at the same time I thought, *where will I go?*

Thinking about it now, I must have had 'doormat' written on my forehead but could not see it then. I cried for days, my tears burning with the sting of betrayal: Mike for lying and squandering our savings and me for forgiving this man who had proven himself to be untrustworthy.

There was nothing else to do at the time but to start saving again for our deposit. I felt sorry for him and really believed that with my help he would be able to stop gambling.

In 1978, I fell pregnant with twins, but unfortunately, I lost half of my pregnancy within three months. That was hard for both of us.

The doctors said that the rest of the pregnancy was going to be okay. Although I was sad that I lost one of the twins, I was so happy about the good news that I was still pregnant. The doctors' instructions were clear: I needed complete rest for a couple of weeks when I got home to ensure the health of my remaining baby. I cannot describe how worried I was for the next six months.

The day after the miscarriage, I returned home from hospital. Mike helped me to unpack and settled me in. Shortly after we got home from hospital, the house phone rang. It was a member of Mike's family telling him that his father had collapsed, was very ill and that he should go there immediately. Mike left me on my own in the flat while he went over to his parents' house to see if he could do anything to help.

When this person called my husband, his father had already died of a heart attack, but he didn't tell Mike until he got there. Two or three hours later, Mike came back with his uncle. As soon as I saw them with their heads down and looking grief-stricken, I just knew. My gut was telling me that my father-in-law had passed away, and I was right. I was devastated by our loss as I was very close to my in-laws. They treated me like my natural parents, which helped me beyond measure since my own parents were living so far away from me. I grieved the loss of my second dad.

Following my father-in-law's funeral, Mike and I moved in with my mother-in-law to support her and look after her. She was devastated by the loss of her beloved husband. They were very close and loving towards each other. It was hard for all of us and even harder for my mother-in-law whose life had changed so dramatically.

As I was pregnant with my son, we all had something positive to look forward to. We stayed with my mother-in-law for six months and saved more for the deposit on a home of our own. By then I was close to the end of my pregnancy, and my mother-in-law started to feel more like herself and cope better as a widow. We wanted to move into our own place. With the money that we had saved again, we put down a deposit on a two-bedroom flat in Wood Green, north London. It wasn't within walking distance, but it wasn't far from my mother-in-law, who we visited on a regular basis. I was so happy and felt lucky to have her. She was a loving and caring mother-in-law. I truly loved her.

After three months in our new flat, on 12 August 1978 at 11pm, I went into labour. My darling son, David, was born at 5:45 am on 13 August 1978, which was also my birthday. Number 13 is unlucky for some, but that day was the happiest day of my life. I had a beautiful and healthy baby. I wanted to have children regardless of what kind of life I had with his dad. I didn't want to feel that I was alone in this country –to be among my own family. My son gave me that. David was the best thing that ever happened to me. I love him dearly.

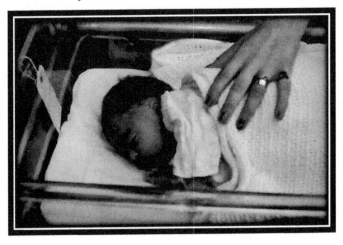

My darling baby, David Louis Shaw.

As soon as I came home from hospital with David, my husband started coming home late from work. It was very hard for me to be in the flat by myself day after day. We were new to the area, and I didn't know anyone. Also, I didn't drive. I relied on a friend from maternity classes to pick me up once a week (or whenever she could) to take me out with my baby for coffee. While I was struggling with long days on my own at home, believing that my husband was working long hours, he was going to the casinos after work to gamble.

I started to question his whereabouts. 'Mike, where have you been? You should have been home from work hours and hours ago. When you disappear for so long, I don't know what you're doing or if you're even alive.'

His excuses (or lies) would vary.

'I got stuck in traffic.'

'No,' I said, 'that doesn't make sense. I called your office at 5:30 pm last night, and they told me that you had already left an hour ago. You came home at three in the morning. Are you telling me that you have been travelling from Hackney to Wood Green for *ten* hours? I don't think so. This behaviour is unacceptable. It must stop and stop right now.'

My concerns and feelings were falling on deaf ears. My husband continued to work, lie and gamble. I was miserable and isolated from the outside world. Not having any family or friends to give me perspective or help me and having a dishonest husband who was gambling was extremely hard.

And it only got more difficult.

Life is a Gamble

Chapter 14

Postnatal Depression

Another baby was born the same day as David to a mother by the name of Jean with whom I became acquainted while we attended antenatal classes. We became good friends. Jean, unfortunately, developed postnatal depression. At the time, I didn't understand how serious depression could be and what it could do to a mother and child if it wasn't addressed properly. I thought that if people had a nice house, car and money, they should be happy. Jean had all of that, but she was not happy.

Jean was depressed and desperate for help. I found out that she, like me, had no family in England or close friends around her. Poor Jean, she couldn't cope with her baby. In deep despair, she started to harm herself by scratching her arms until they bled. Whether on the telephone or in person, she would cry and pour out her anguish and desperation to me.

I set aside my problems with my lying, gambling husband and tried to help her as much as I could by going to her house with my baby during the day until her husband got home from work. I kept myself busy by making up bottles for her baby, making sure she would eat, and talking about whatever was on her mind. We also talked a lot on the phone. After a few months, I saw little improvement in how she felt. I realised that she needed professional help.

I urged her and her husband to go to her GP and ask for that much-needed help. They went. The doctor put her on some kind of medication, and she also received intensive counselling. She was very quickly on the road to recovery. Jean started to enjoy her beautiful baby and life in general. I was so happy for her and pleased that I was there when she most needed someone to help her, listen to her and not judge her.

It was then that I discovered the power of counselling and my affinity for it, but it would be years later until I could get formal training to become a counsellor. I've always wanted to help less fortunate people than myself, and this seemed a perfect way to do just that. But I also knew that after talking to troubled people, I tended to carry their problems home with me, and that wasn't healthy. I knew I needed help to help people, so in 1990, I enrolled in an intensive, one-year counselling course with the Centre for the Advancement of Counselling.

I decided to do the counselling course for two different reasons. First, I wanted to help decrease my daily stress by improving my marriage and help my husband stop gambling. After a while, I realised that the only person in this situation I could help (or change) was me. Second, I was ready to change my career completely to do something less stressful than housekeeping. I knew I wanted to be in management, so I could use my counselling skills to help my staff and colleagues with management stress so they could be happier, healthier and more productive in their work. Having experienced personal and work problems of my own, I fully understood and sympathised with a wide range of emotional issues.

In this course, I learned how to cope with difficult emotional situations and gained psychological knowledge to help me deal with various situations. I also was trained on giving proper advice to people less fortunate than myself, and, at the same time, I gained valuable insights about helping myself. After completing the course, I obtained the Diploma for Advance Counselling skills. I have used these skills throughout my life.

***

Within a year, Jean had fully recovered and was happy again with her baby, herself, and life. I was happy for her and her little family. Jean and I remained good friends for the next couple of years. Unfortunately, after two years they decided to go back to their native country with their baby boy so she could be near her family. We kept in touch for a while by writing letters (her family did not have a house phone), but the letters came less and less frequently. I missed her terribly. She was the only close friend that I had at the time. Just as she was in a position to return the favour I had done for her, she was gone, and I was still stuck dealing with my marital problems alone. I had to believe that I was blessed with health and strength to get on with my life and sort out my problems all on my own.

After Jean left the UK, my home situation got worse by the day. My husband was in the casinos gambling most nights until early morning. He was notable to keep up with mortgage repayments. I couldn't take being isolated at home with a young child anymore. This man was tormenting me. One minute he would insult me by saying I was a peasant and too skinny, that nobody would want me. The next day he would tell me he loved me and couldn't live without me. He was like Dr Jekyll and Mr

Hyde. Life was bloody awful most of the time whil e living with him, but I had nowhere to go with my little boy. was a wretched existence.

One winter morning, before he went to work, he put a piece of paper in the kitchen bin. Then, he took it out of that bin and put that piece of paper in the bin liner outside the front door when he left for work. I became suspicious After he had gone, I rummaged through that snow-covered bin, found that piece of paper and took it out of the bin liner. I scrutinised it but was not entirely sure what it was.

I called the number that was on the piece of paper. The company confirmed that it was a lending agency. Mr and Mrs Mike Shaw borrowed money from them, and I was holding the receipt proving it –both signatures included.

Oh, my God! I was rendered speechless for a few moments. Then I told them, 'I don't know anything about any loans. I didn't agree to borrow money and certainly didn't sign any documents. There must be some mistake. 'I was trembling so much that I could barely keep the telephone receiver close to my face.

The gentleman from that company said in a sympathetic voice, 'I am sorry to hear this Ma'am, but there is no mistake. Your husband told us that you couldn't come to our office because your baby wasn't well, and he got you to sign the form. If what you are telling me is that your husband lied to you and forged your signature, we will need to report the matter to the police. He can end up in prison. This is a very serious matter. 'His voice sounded firm, stern.

I begged him, 'Please, don't do or say anything until I've talked to my husband. I promise I'll call back tomorrow with an explanation. Will you do that for me, please?' I'm sure he could hear me sniffling back my tears and runny nose.

'I suppose one day will not make a big difference. So, yes, I will wait for your call. But I expect it first thing in the morning,' he said. Then, with a kinder voice, he added, 'Try not to get too overwrought, Ma'am. If what you say is true, you have not done anything wrong.'

'Thank you, Sir. Thank you.'

During that day, my husband telephoned me at home many times. It was like he had a feeling that something was not right.

When he came home, I asked him as calmly as I could because he was holding sixteen-month-old David in his arms, 'How much money did you borrow?'

At first, his eyes widened, and his mouth fell open. He just stared at me. Then, his neck, face, and head turned crimson while his body tensed up. 'What money?' He asked too loudly.

David started squirming. Mike paused for a minute, looking down at the floor. In a more measured voice, he asked, 'Did they phone you?'

'Who?'

He sighed, 'The company I've borrowed money from.'

I told him, 'No, I called them.'

He was close to dropping my darling baby son out of his arms and onto the floor. Instead, David just slipped through his arms.

When he realised that the baby was safe on the floor, my husband fell to his knees and told me, 'I didn't forge your signature. Two weeks ago, I gave you a blank piece of paper to sign and lied about what it was for.'

What a fool I was to trust him, knowing by then that he was a compulsive gambler and not to be believed.

He continued, 'I told them that we agreed to borrow £5,000.'

That was a lot of money then (and now), especially since I was not working. He was gambling with money that we didn't have.

I asked him, 'What did you borrow money for?'

He said, 'I'm behind with the mortgage repayment, and I thought that by borrowing this money I would catch up with mortgage repayments. I would pay this loan through my bank account, and you would be none the wiser.'

'Great, and what now?' I asked him.

He was crying his eyes out and said, 'If you tell them that you had nothing to do with this loan, I'll go to prison for a long time, lose my job, the house and my life won't be worth living without you and our son.'

There he was again, looking for sympathy. He got us into this mess and was telling me that I had the responsibility of saving him! My relationship felt like a puzzle with no solution. I didn't know whether to laugh or cry.

'Please, Dee, forgive me. I love you so much. I promise never to gamble again. And this time I mean it! If I ever gamble after this, you can leave me and take David with you. I deserve to be alone and you deserve someone better than me. But just give me one more chance, Dee. Please?'

They say inaction is a form of action. By not leaving Mike then and there, I made chose to stay. And he knew it.

'Please, please call the loan company, and tell them that there has been some misunderstanding and that you are okay with it now.'

I nodded.

He smiled.

I fixed what he had broken by calling the loan company the following day and telling them what Mike suggested I say. The immediate threat to our family was avoided. But a more profound, sinister danger was brewing. Mike wasn't only gambling with our money; he was gambling with me. He was betting that I wouldn't leave him. And, so far, it was a sure bet. I was beginning to worry, however, that I, too, was gambling with something quite precious: my son and me. Would life be better with Mike in our lives or without him? Little boys need their fathers, but what kind of father was Mike? And what about me? I had lost my positive, independent self in this difficult marriage. I had just lied for my husband. Feeling sorry for someone is not the same as loving them, is it? Did he love me or was he using me? I spent many a sleepless night in distress over what to do.

Mike must have been aware of my pensive mood after I lied for him. A few days later, he suggested that he use some of the loan money to pay for an airline ticket to bring my mother over from Serbia to look after the baby so that we could both work hard to pay off the loan. After we caught up with the mortgage repayments, we could move to a bigger house. He always managed to paint a sunny picture of the future, assuming I would forget about the gloomy past. His sure bet came through again. I agreed to go along with his plan, especially since it involved seeing my mother after all these years.

I loved my mother for agreeing to come over to help us out. She left her husband and the rest of the family behind in Serbia even though they needed her help over there, too. *What a mess she'll be walking into*, I thought. But I believed my husband when he promised that things would get better before my Mum returned to Serbia.

Nothing stopped my mother from coming over to give us a much-needed pair of helping hands; she loved David and me whole heartedly. When she arrived, I felt safe for a while. Having Mum living with us would, I believed, stop his gambling. I was wrong yet again.

My mother didn't speak English at all, but she was happy to come over to help us out and look after her grandson so that we could stand on our feet again financially. I don't know how my mother coped day after day, for nine months (on her own during weekdays), with the baby who was only seventeen-months-old when she arrived. David was so young that she couldn't even talk with him.

Although my mother didn't understand what Mike and I were saying to each other, she could see from the expressions on our faces that neither of us was happy. She was heartbroken to see me suffering in a bad marriage but couldn't do more than she was already doing. She certainly couldn't stay with us longer than nine months. She went back home worrying about her little grandson and us.

Selfishly, I was devastated to see my mother go back home. I felt it wasn't just my mother who had left me but my best friend, too. I was so worried to be left alone with this man who was spending hours and hours in the casinos and betting shops while I sat at home with my baby worrying about everything. His gambling was going from bad to worse– three to four nights a week he wouldn't come home until the early hours of the morning.

I should have known better; a leopard never changes its spots. Mike didn't stop gambling before or after my mother left. It's tragic that I didn't understand about compulsive gambling when I first met him. I was oblivious to how destructive the lying and irrational craving to gamble could be to everyone around those afflicted with this condition. All the love and good intentions I could muster would never change him. I see that now; I didn't then.

Something had to change. But what? And how?

Chapter 15

Addiction Has Many Victims

When Mike won money, he was ecstatic. I became his princess. He would tell me how lucky he was to have me as his wife. But when he lost money (which was most of the time), I was the worst peasant and should go back to the gutter where I came from. This went on for nine months after my mother left. I couldn't take it anymore.

I decided to find a registered childminder to look after our son full-time and went back to work as the Head Housekeeper in a five-star hotel in central London. Doing my job well was a challenge for several reasons. Being Head Housekeeper in such a luxurious hotel was a demanding position requiring a great deal of responsibility, organisation and effort. I couldn't fully concentrate on my job because of my constant worries about the welfare of my son and guilt about leaving him in the care of a stranger. In addition, I was exhausted from too many sleepless nights waiting for my husband to come home or wondering *if* he would come home. I didn't know which would be worse. When he eventually did come home, it was mostly in the early hours of the next morning. I couldn't relax and go to sleep. I often went to work exhausted and was struggling with my job.

My husband agreed to drop off our son to the minder in the morning, and after a long, challenging day at work, I would pick him up. No matter how drained I was, nothing felt burdensome where my son was concerned. David was the one bright light in an otherwise drab existence. If it weren't for my darling boy, I might not have had the will to survive that time in my life. I gave him life, and he gave me the strength to live.

The first childminder didn't work out. My son was two-and-a-half-years-old. After a couple of weeks, I pulled David out. I felt she was too strict with children. The next childminder was from Ireland. She had a strong Northern Ireland accent. When I met her, my first reaction was, *oh, no! Not another Bridget!* But I had to give her a chance.

David told me, 'Mama when Auntie Karen shouts, I wet my pants.'

'Oh, Sweetie, does she clean you up and change your clothes for you?' I cradled him in my arms and rocked him back and forth.

'No, Mama. She just yells some more and asks me why I had to wet my pants...in front of everyone!' He buried his head in my shoulder. My sweet little David was so afraid of her that every time I was about to leave him with her (Mike often fell asleep and 'forgot' our arrangement) or picked him up, he started crying as soon as we got in the car, and repeated, 'I don't like Auntie Karen. I don't want to stay with her, please, Mama, *please!*'

I felt like such a terrible mother by not protecting my precious son from such a harsh child minder. At the same time, I had to continue to work to pay the mortgage to save the roof over our heads. And it was difficult to find another registered child minder. I wanted my child to look forward to his day, not dread it. My son had enough problems being with his parents who were arguing all the time. He needed a respite from stress, not more of it. I was always very protective of my son, so I decided to speak to childminder about it. Either we would sort things out for my son and the other children, so everyone could be in a pleasant environment, or I would take my son away from her and leave my job to be with David until I found someone else that was suitable for my son.

When I brought up the subject up, she said, 'Dee, I'm sorry. I don't shout. This is how I talk.'

I raised my eyebrows. Then I asked, 'Is it possible that we talk further about this over a cup of tea?'

'Of course, Dee!'

The very next day we met to talk.

During our conversation, Karen opened up to me. 'Please don't tell anyone this, but I think one of the reasons I might be raising my voice from time to time is because my husband is an alcoholic. 'She folded and unfolded her napkin.

My eyes widened, but she wasn't looking at me. All I said was, 'I understand. 'I reached over and patted her arm.

'Dee, I'm just so unhappy most of the time. I know I've been abrupt with the children, and that's wrong. You're not the first mum to raise concerns. I will sort this out. I'm so sorry. 'She looked at me with the teary eyes of a trapped woman.

Karen reassured me that she would take on board what I'd said regarding my concerns. She also explained that her husband only drank when all the children had gone home.

A few days later I opened up and shared my problem with her. 'Karen, do you remember when I told you that I understood your situation with your alcoholic husband?'

She nodded slowly. 'Is your husband an alcoholic, too?'

I smiled and shook my head. 'No. But just as bad. He's a compulsive gambler. I'm terribly unhappy, too. That's why I went back to work. I can put all my problems behind me for a little while. Yes, they are all waiting there for me when I walk through my front door, but I try to be strong for myself and my darling son.'

'Yes, I thought having lovely children round me all day would be enough to lift my spirits and remind me of the goodness in life. But I feel like I'm surrounded by a thick cloud of black smoke that's choking the life out of me.'

'I know exactly how you feel. It's too easy to lose yourself in *their* addiction. Other people don't know how we feel, but they can see how we look and behave. And, believe me, once you start behaving like a strong, positive woman, you'll begin to feel strong and positive again.'

Our conversations led to a friendship. Because I felt comfortable with her, I suggested that she attend some counselling if possible. I told her, 'It *will* help you to feel better. Then you will enjoy the work and the children that you are getting paid to look after. 'I also told her that if I didn't attend counselling for our marriage and his gambling, I probably would have ended up in the psychiatric hospital as a patient.

Karen was grateful for my suggestions to her. She contacted *Relate* counselling organisation and received help from them for the next six months. From then on, she spoke softly, took the children on outings more often, and even smiled more. Everyone was much happier. My son would tell me that Auntie Karen was not shouting now and that he was looking forward to going there. That gave me peace of mind to carry on with my job without having to worry about him being traumatised.

I was proud of myself for confronting my son's childminder problem with directness, diplomacy, and compassion. I discovered that nearly any message could be delivered in a way that it will be received constructively if it's delivered with the right intention and in the right way. Armed with this discovery, I began to be stronger coping with my own problems. I decided that the next person I needed to speak to was my husband.

One night after I put our son to bed, we sat down.

I took a deep breath and said calmly, 'Mike, I don't know about you, but I'm not very happy with the way things are. I don't appreciate being bullied and insulted by you when you're in a bad mood.'

'Oh, please. Can't you just let me relax?' He looked away from me.

'No, Mike. This is important. Look at me. I've asked you a thousand times get professional help to stop your gambling. But you never take me seriously.'

'Yes, I do. I've tried. It just doesn't work. It's in my blood or something. Don't nag, Dee. 'He sighed.

I took another deep breath. 'Listen, Mike, I'm serious. Either get yourself into some professional program for compulsive gamblers, or you have leave the matrimonial home. The choice is yours. Our son needs to have one proper and stable parent rather than one and a half. That half is you right now.'

Mike's eyes widened and his breathing quickened. When he spoke, his voice was louder and sharper than usual. 'You know I've been trying for years to quit. This is harder on me than it is on you, so stop acting like you're the one who's the victim.'

I hadn't expected that and didn't have a reply.

He suggested that I go with him to Gamblers Anonymous to support him.

I agreed.

When we arrived at the meeting, he told me that he would go into a separate room where the men were. I should go with the ladies in another room where I would get support from them as they were in the same situation as I was. It made sense to me. I was willing to do anything to help him stop gambling and salvage what was left of our marriage. I made up my mind that this was the last chance for both of us, and I very much wanted him to stop gambling for all our sakes.

Believing that he would stop gambling with the help of this internationally-recognised program, I agreed to go with him once a week to support him. I behaved like women who love too much and who believe miracles happen, addictions disappear and stories end with 'happily ever after. 'Yet again, I couldn't have been more wrong.

My first night at Gamblers Anonymous was my last. I was led to a spacious meeting room and introduced to between ten to fifteen other wives who were in a similar situation to mine. I was shocked by what I heard from them and what kind of things they were going through on a daily basis.

These women shared story after story of stealing household money for gambling, abusive behaviour, womanising, their husbands staying out until the wee hours of the morning or disappearing for days, lying, bullying, and moodiness to the point of terrorising the entire household. Except for the womanising, they could have been describing Mike. When it was my time to 'share,' that is what I told them.

I didn't tell these wives of compulsive gamblers that I heard more that evening than I could cope with. What I was looking forward to and wanted to hear from any of those wives was that their husbands had stopped gambling. I wanted to know what measures they had taken to help them stop gambling and for them to tell me that they were attending the meeting to help and support others.

Unfortunately, and to my surprise, that was not the case. Those wives were there to tell their stories of woe to others who understood in the hopes of learning how to live with a gambler. And they were happy to do so. *Not me,* I thought. *I do not want to learn how to live with a gambler. I need to learn how to live without one.* The only thing I learnt at that meeting was: once a gambler, always a gambler.

While these groups may be therapeutic for many people, I found their aim very upsetting and discouraging. After that very first meeting, I decided that I was not going back. What I needed to do (and did) was to bring our son up on my own.

When we came out of that meeting, my husband asked me, 'What did you think about the meeting?'

It was dark so that he couldn't see my face, but I'm sure he could hear the anger in my words. 'I am not going to be fooled and suffer anymore living in a cuckoo land like those women are in there! They want to learn how to live with a gambler. Not me! I want gambling out of my life for good. That means you need to get out of my life and our matrimonial home. I deserve a normal life, and that doesn't include you!'

A week later, before he left us, he said that he wanted to share the furniture from our flat. One of the things he wanted to take with him was the fridge. He warned me that if I didn't pay him for it, he would take it into storage. If I didn't agree in writing to repay the rest of the loan that he had borrowed, then he wouldn't leave. He also told me I would have to apply for a court order to get him out. *How nasty,* I thought. He didn't need the fridge as he moved in with his mother.

I was furious with him. 'How could you take the fridge that I use to keep food and milk for our boy? You know I don't have the money to pay you for it! 'My voice trembled with rage.

'That's your problem, not mine. Just make sure I get paid for it, or it's gone. 'His voice was unusually calm.

One of my friends loaned me the money, and I paid him to keep the fridge.

I agreed to pay for both the loan and the fridge, and we separated. I kept the receipt from 1982 for the fridge. It reads: 'received £110.00 in respect of one fridge which now belongs to Mrs Dee S and will be left at 144 Maryland Road when I leave.' Signed by Mike S.

I was ready to be done with this man. But he had different plans.

Life is a Gamble

Chapter 16

Love is Blind and so Was I

After he left us, Mike realised what he lost and kept phoning every day and writing me letters every day, putting them through my letterbox. He told me that he missed our son and me. He needed us as much as the grass needs water. His life was not worth living without us. He kept begging me to give him one last chance and take him back.

Yes, you are singing the same song again. But, NO chance, Mister, I thought. But my resolve wavered. During his absence, I sorted myself out, got a new part-time job and employed a young girl by the name of Tracey who was also working part-time to take my son to the childminder in the morning. I would pick him up at midday when I finished work. This worked very well.

During our separation, he told me in the letters that he was attending Gamblers Anonymous, getting help and had vowed gambling was a thing of the past. He also promised that he would do everything in his power to make his family happy. If I had him back, he would buy a house, and I would not have to work again. He would make sure (this time) to keep me and our boy happy. The pressure from him was too great yet again. I fell for it. Like a fool, I gave in. I wanted to believe that he loved David and me enough to change or that our love was enough to change him. Being a good wife and mother was important to me, and being a single parent was demanding.

He moved back with us three months later on 13 August, for my son's and my birthday.

He kept his word for a while, but my happiness was short-lived.

When we got back together, Mike bought one flat in North London and one in Bournemouth that overlooked the sea. The house in London was for us to live in. Both of those properties were bought through mortgages. To sweeten the deal, he got me a brand-new car that was bought on hire purchase. I don't know where he got the money to buy his way back into our family, but that's what he did.

All was well for four years, and I was happy during that time. Then the trouble started. Again. Mike started making excuses that he needed to work longer hours to earn extra money to repay the mortgages. But I knew in my heart something had shifted back to the 'old Mike. 'He had started to gamble again, betting on horses during the day and going to the casino after work. The familiar pattern of coming home in the early hours of the morning re-emerged.

Because I didn't want to believe he had fallen back into his old ways and I didn't have any solid proof that he was gambling again, I chose to believe that he was telling me the truth. He was so desperate to have our son and me back in his life, so I decided to turn a blind eye and let him get on with it.

He kept up with the mortgage repayments for all of the properties. Our fridge was always full of food. His mood was fairly stable. On the surface, everything seemed relatively fine. But I felt it was far from fine. And I was never good at hiding my feelings.

Mike would often ask me, 'Dee, what's your problem?'

'Oh, nothing.'

'Nothing! Bah! You have everything. A nice house, nice car. Just relax. Everything is fine,' he would say. Sometimes he would wink. Sometimes he would walk away.

Sometimes I would relax, believing that he was just working hard; other times, my anxiety would rise to the surface, and I'd complain about something petty which lead to more bickering. Afterwards, I kept thinking that he was right. *I did have everything. We are getting on well, going on nice holidays. What more did I want?* I told myself just to stop worrying and give him a chance as he was working very hard to give us a good life just as he promised. *He's right,* I told myself. *Just relax.*

He sold the flat in North London that he bought during our separation. We were both working, he persuaded me that, together, we should take out a mortgage to buy two semi-detached houses next to each other in Southgate, North London.

I was never comfortable buying anything on credit. My parents taught me that I should only spend what I have money to buy. They also emphasised that I respect and support my mother-in-law. She and I always got on so well, we felt like mother and daughter. She had no daughters, and my parents were in another country. And she absolutely adored my son, her only grandson.

For this reason, in1987 I suggested that my mother-in-law move in with us. My husband then proposed that we sell the two houses and buy a bigger home for all of us to share. We were all getting on well with each other, so his proposal seemed reasonable.

Mike changed his mind about selling the two semi-detached houses. He wanted to let them to tenants, instead. He planned to make money on the rent and sell them later when there would be some equity earned on them. All the money from monthly rent and the sale, he said, would be used to pay down the mortgage on the new home. When we spoke to his mum, she was all for it. We were all looking forward to moving in together.

But it was a mistake. A big one.

When we decided to move into the new house, I gave up work so I could be available to set up our new home and look after my nine-year-old son and my mother-in-law. Mike was all for it, saying he would handle all of the finances.

'How are you going to do that?' I was confused as I knew he had just declared bankruptcy for the second time since we had been married.

'I have a plan, Dee. We'll put the new house in Mum's and your name, but my name will be on the mortgage.'

'Can you do that...legally?'

'Sure. It's done all the time. 'He was so confident.

'But how will you make the monthly repayments without income from me? And can you get a loan if you're bankrupt?' I was very sceptical.

He gave me a hard look, the one I had seen many times before that said, *enough!* Then he cleared his throat and said in a patronising voice, 'Relax, Dee. I know what I'm doing. You take care of the family. I'll take care of the money.'

I don't know how he managed to get the mortgage whilst bankrupt. But in those days, anyone could have borrowed more than they were earning from a bank/building society – all they needed was a letter from their employer and a verbal reference. Mike's firm must have provided false information for his earnings. Or he manufactured it on their stationery.

In June 1988, we all moved into a five-bedroom house. We were all delighted. His half of the house was then transferred into my name. A couple of months after we moved in, things between Mike and me went sour. Again. He became meaner than ever towards me. By Christmas, he stopped paying the mortgage. Mike was away more than he was at home. The excuses for his absences returned. Everything was familiar except that now I suspected that, in addition to gambling, he might also be cheating on me with another woman.

I was right.

One weekend he went to France. When he got back, he brought me one-and-a-half underwear sets.

'That's nice, but where is the other piece of this set?' I dangled it in front of him.

Mike shrugged, turned his attention back to reading the newspaper and mumbled, 'In the boot of my car.'

I went straight out to check. The boot of the car was absolutely empty. I marched inside and told him, 'No, it's not. The boot is empty.'

He never even looked up from the newspaper. 'Huh. It was there.'

Two days later, he brought it to me.

I always believed that Mike would rather spend time and money on gambling than on having a mistress. But, I could think of no other reason that part of an underwear set was missing for two days other than that underwear was with another woman. It wasn't exactly proof, but seeds of doubt about his fidelity had been planted.

In August 1988, David (who was ten) and I went to Serbia for my brother's wedding. We stayed there with my family for a month. My husband took this as an opportunity and insisted I give him power of attorney to sell the two houses and release equity from them to decrease the mortgage on the new house we all lived in.

Our relationship was a mess, and I didn't trust him. 'No, Mike. Any decisions about selling properties has to wait until I get back from my holiday. I want to be sure that the proceeds will be paid into the building society to decrease the new mortgage. As we agreed.'

When he got angry, the veins round his head would protrude and pulse. I could tell he was quite cross when he shouted at me,' You don't trust me! When will you do so? I am fed up with it!' After pacing round a bit, he collected himself and tried a different approach. 'All right,' he said more calmly, 'if you don't trust me, will you give power of attorney to our solicitor?' He was our good friend at the time.

I agreed just to get him off my back, thinking the houses couldn't be sold as any transaction required my signature. So, off I went on holiday.

When David and I got back from Serbia, my husband wouldn't talk to me. When I pleaded with him to tell me what was going on, all he said was, 'Just to let you know, the two houses have been sold, and there was no equity in either of them.'

I didn't believe him as we had those houses for six months, the monthly mortgage was regularly paid and house prices were going up fast at that time. The next morning, I looked in his wardrobe. I discovered that he had taken most of his clothes. A sick feeling roiled in the pit of my stomach. I began looking round the house. Many of his belongings were gone, too.

I went back to my bedroom to think. As I paced, my breaths grew quicker and shallower. *Oh, my God, he's leaving us. How am I going to manage financially? I have to get a job. I have to bring up my son on my own! And what is going to happen to my mother-in-law who's old and disabled? Is he just going to leave us in this big house to fend for ourselves? How could he?* I had far from a perfect marriage, but I wasn't prepared for this.

The next morning my husband went to work without saying goodbye. A few hours later, I called him to ask what was going on and where the rest of his clothes had gone. He told me that while I was away, he had been thinking. He had decided that we couldn't live together anymore and that we needed to talk. He did not want to upset his mother more than she already was, so we arranged to meet on neutral ground. We met in a pub car park in Golders Green, North London.

As soon as we sat down on benches opposite each other, he looked at me straight in my eyes and said, 'I don't love you anymore. I've met someone else, and I'll be moving out of the house tonight.'

'What did you just say?' I asked. 'Did I hear it right that you have met someone else, and that's why you're leaving us?'

'Yes, you heard that right.'

I held both hands to my stomach. For the second time in two days, I felt a burning, sharp pain in the middle of my belly – as if someone had stabbed me. I knew he lied and gambled, but I never thought he would cheat on me or abandon his family.

'But you said I was the only one you ever loved…' I knew it was irrational, but I felt the ultimate betrayal by this man who had been a horrible husband.

'Well, that's not true anymore. 'He could have been talking to a stranger. His voice was flat, emotionless.

Perhaps it was the callousness of his voice or the insult of being so casually discarded after years of tolerating the insanity he brought to my life, but something shifted in me. Or, instead, a quality in me that I never knew existed emerged and took over. And it was not pretty.

Life is a Gamble

Chapter 17

We Won the War but Lost the Peace
Serbian Proverb

Mike had nothing more to say to me, not even 'goodbye. 'As he got up to leave, I watched him and thought, *I hate him. He has made my life a living nightmare. He doesn't deserve one minute of happiness.*

When he got into his car to leave, that hidden part of me took over. I got in my car and decided to drive into his car to hurt him. At the time, I wanted him dead, and I didn't care about the consequences. My life felt worthless. Hopeless. I tried a few times to drive into his car, but he managed to dodge twice. I missed him both times.

Thank God I did not succeed in my mission. Who knows what would have happened to either of us? My much-loved son would have been the real victim. That was never my intention.

As I was in shock and still enraged, I drove my car straight into the main road without checking for oncoming traffic. I was extremely lucky that I didn't hurt or kill anyone or myself while I was in that state of mind. Mike drove off without looking back to see if his son's mother was okay or not. All he seemed to care about was himself and his new love.

While driving home, I sobbed. I repeated aloud, 'All I wanted was a happy family for our son and for his mum who needed our help. Why wasn't that enough? Why?'

Then I began blaming myself for reconciling with him after our separation and putting our son through all this chaos. *Why did I do it?* I asked myself. *Just to confuse the child who didn't ask to be born?*

When David came home from school, I was quiet. Worried about breaking the news to him that his dad was going to leave us for someone else that same evening, I rehearsed different, gentle ways of telling him. Nothing seemed right, so I didn't say anything.

When my ex-husband came home from work, he told our son and his mother what he was about to do. David was flustered. He started to cry and ran upstairs to his bedroom. This perturbed me so much that my rage re-emerged. *That bastard isn't just betraying and abandoning me, he's throwing sweet David and his dear mum away like garbage, too!*

It was entirely out of my usual character, but I became violent towards him. I stopped for a moment and thought, *how can I hurt him?* I knew what I was about to do. I became as strong as a lioness. Then I went wild.

We had a few heavy plant pots in our hallway. I picked them up, one by one, aimed and threw them with all my might at Mike's bald head.

I missed every time. Instead of hitting him, the pots smashed against the wall. After I calmed down, I saw what a mess I had made, but not as much of a mess as I would have made if I had hit my target. My poor aim was a good thing; I was capable of anger but not manslaughter.

I will always be grateful to Mike for one thing. He did not call 999 to ask for emergency services, like the police, an ambulance or a crisis team. He could have told them that I had gone off the rails. That I was a threat to everyone in the house and myself, too. If he had done that, I probably would have been taken to a local psychiatric unit which would have made me even angrier.

I can understand how easy it is to be labelled as mentally ill while people are in distress. I was not ill – I was devastated and overwhelmed. My life felt as if it was spinning out of control. I panicked that I would never find solid ground again.

During the fight with Mike, my young son was upstairs in his bedroom. My mother-in-law was downstairs in the lounge. Both were behind closed doors while all of the pottery-smashing was going on. Thank God they didn't witness it, but I'm sure that they heard the commotion. I can only imagine the fear and anxiety they both must have felt listening to the hysteria.

When David came out of his bedroom, I took him out in the car and drove off in anger. I drove a short distance from the house to the roundabout but then decided to go back to the house to confront Mike again. Again, my rage took over.

I drove at full speed towards the house and surrounding wall…with my son in the car. I was shaking, my fists clenching the steering wheel. The only thought going through my mind was, *I have nothing to live for and so I might just as well end it all.*

Just before I reached the wall, my son shouted, 'Mum! Please! PLEASE! Stop! Stop the car!'

His precious voice broke through the nonsense in my confused mind. I slammed my foot on the brake. At the speed I was going, I would have killed or crippled us both. Instead, the car just touched the wall with minor damage. I wept into my trembling hands.

'I'm so sorry...so sorry, David. I...I didn't mean...I would never...so selfish...so sorry...you're everything. I love you. You know that?' I tried to pull myself together for my son's sake.

He surprised me. He was more composed than any ten-year-old should be in a situation like that. Not only did my darling son realise what I was about to do and manage to stop me in time, but he grabbed my hand and told me, 'Everything's going to be all right, Mum.'

And I believed him.

Mike was still in the house, standing by the window holding his head. He witnessed the whole thing. I wonder if he felt any responsibility for any of it. I still feel a profound sense of guilt about putting my sweet son through that horrible experience.

I wish now that I had taken my son's hand, walked out without the car and stayed out until his father left the house. I can't go back or dwell on what I could have done differently, but what I can do is share the experience, as embarrassing and upsetting as it is to me, in the hopes that others might use it as a cautionary tale.

Fifteen minutes later, my husband left home. Within ten minutes, the phone rang. It was Mike. He called to speak to our son. He told him, 'Sorry boy, but I have to leave home as I can't live with your mum anymore.'

He did not tell him the truth; that he was leaving us all to move in with his mistress. He also told our son, 'Please remember, I will always be there for you.'

Again, Mike lied. While our son was growing up, his father was out there somewhere but hardly saw him while he was at school or university. He didn't support David emotionally or financially.

Mike may not have plotted to harm us, but he did hurt us in various and lasting ways while he lived with us. Once I adjusted to the idea that he was out of our lives for good by his choice, I thought that we (David, my mother-in-law and I) could start fresh and begin the healing process.

I should have known better.

Chapter 18

A Shaky New Start

The solicitor 'friend' who Mike got to draw up my Power of Attorney documents turned out to be just as dishonest as Mike. I did not see this person before I went on holiday to Serbia or sign any papers to say that I'd agreed for the houses to be sold while I was away. Between them, they forged my signature and sold both houses. I was never given access to the records of the sales to determine what, if any, profit came from the transactions. Mike's claim that there was no equity in either house seemed like just another lie, but I was powerless to prove otherwise.

When Mike left, I tried contacting this solicitor and was told each time that he was out of the office. Eventually, I reached him. He was quite cordial. 'Please come to my office, Dee. We'll clear everything up for you.'

I got to his office and sat in front of his desk.

'Before we talk about the sale, could you please sign this for me?' His smile was broad and emotionless. He slid a piece of paper in front of me to sign.

I gave him a questioning look.

'Don't worry. It's just a formality. You know. Before we talk business. 'He pushed a pen in my direction.

After all I had been through, the smart thing to do would have been to read it. But no, not trusting Dee. 'If you need this so I can find out what happened to that house, then okay. 'I trusted him as a good friend and signed that piece of paper.

I was about to ask him to explain when he looked at his watch and said, 'Oh, no, Dee. I forgot that I have another appointment. I'm very sorry, but we will have to reschedule. Call back tomorrow, okay? I'm sorry about this, Dee. 'He escorted me out of his office quickly.

After that meeting, the solicitor never answered my calls. I went to his office a few times. Each time I was told he was not there. I have not seen or spoken to him since. He probably had me sign a power of attorney that day in the office.

After Mike left our house, he paid the mortgage for the next two or three months. Then he stopped. My mother-in-law and I were not made aware of this. Because he had been handling the finances, we weren't focused on the mortgage repayments. And we certainly hadn't discussed the terms of our separation or eventual divorce.

Around Christmas time, we received the first letter from the building society to inform us that we were behind with the mortgage repayments by two months. Unless next month's mortgage instalment was paid in full, our house would be repossessed. My mother-in-law and I were quite concerned. I wasn't working, and his mum had put all her savings (£100,000) into that house. How could we keep our comfortable home if there was no money available for us to continue with the mortgage repayments? I couldn't sleep or eat properly. The anxiety was heightened by the fact that neither of us knew about how to sort any of this out.

However, I was advised by a friend who went through a similar situation to go without any delay and register with the local housing department. I put all three of us on the homeless waiting list for accommodation. We were on the waiting list for the next seven months.

During that time, the housing department offered us a one-bedroom accommodation for the three of us in a hostel that was far away from Barnet, North London. We were supposed to share the living room, bathroom and kitchen with other homeless people. I went to see it. While visiting, I met some drunk people. Some of them were smoking cannabis. The whole place stank. *No, I thought, I will not be bringing up my son in such an environment.*

I told my housing officer that the hostel was not an option for us. Our housing officer knew that my mother-in-law was disabled. She had to take her artificial leg off every night before going to bed. Neither David nor I had seen her without her prosthetic. I pointed this out and explained to the housing officer that it would be very distressing for my son and me to witness this and live in one room 24-hours a day for any length of time. The negative impact on all of us of would be profound.

While we were waiting for another accommodation, none of us wanted to be uprooted. David, who was eleven, wanted desperately to remain in his school with his friends. For him to be sent out of the catchment area of his school would have been very upsetting for him. He needed stability, not more upheaval.

So, we stayed in our house and waited for suitable accommodation. Seven months passed. We were still living in the house, but the monthly mortgage was not being paid. How long would they let us stay there? The uncertainty was eating away at me.

One Friday, two burly bailiffs came to the house to inform us that the following Monday – in two days –we would have to vacate the property. They were coming to change the front door lock. I panicked that we had to leave so quickly without knowing where we would go, but at least the waiting and wondering was over.

'What?' I asked. 'Where are we going to live?'

'It's not our problem, Ma'am,' one of them said. 'We are only doing our job. 'He wasn't unkind, just honest. And a bit blunt.

Although it felt like we were being rushed out of the house, we had lived in that big, expensive house for free for nine months (two months of Mike not paying the mortgage and seven months of waiting for the Housing Authority to relocate us). I understood that the Building Society (from whom we got the loan) was losing money on it by not being able to sell the property. The housing authority had been given six months to re-house us, but they weren't able to find us suitable accommodation in that time.

'Excuse me, Sir,' I addressed one of the bailiffs. 'What should I do with the furniture and all our belongings? And what about my disabled mother-in-law and a young child?

They can't be without a proper home.' A tear rolled down my cheek.

They were not interested one bit in my pathetic situation. One of the men said, 'You had six months to sort yourselves out. We're bailiffs. We're here to do our job and get you and your family off this property on Monday whatever happens. 'He also said, 'If you're still here on Monday at 2pm, we'll put you and your furniture outside the property before we change the lock. If you refuse to leave, we'll use force and physically throw you all out of the house. That's our job. 'And they left.

I couldn't believe what was happening to us. I felt I was watching a horror movie. Things were going from bad to worse for us by the minute. My mother-in-law and I were as frightened as woodland animals in a forest fire.

What was going to happen? We had nowhere to go. I was terrified but didn't show this to either of them. On Monday, my son went to school. I hated thinking about telling him what was going to happen when he returned from school, so I didn't. But there was every possibility that Mum and I could be outside the house with all our furniture when David returned from school.

Life is a Gamble

My mum-in-law and I decided not to say anything to David (who we both wanted to protect) until I sorted something out. He had enough to cope with: his dad had left him, we were losing our home, and he had just advanced from the infants to junior school. Now we were moving to some unknown place. Mum and I thought enough was enough. If we could shelter him from at least this stress, we wanted to try.

As I had already been on the housing waiting list for six months without being able to get suitable accommodation, I telephoned my housing officer. I was in tears but also very angry. I shouted at him, blaming him for not trying harder to sort us out and for letting us get into a crisis situation. I must say the housing officer was sympathetic and pointed out to me, in a very calm manner, that I had an hour to get to Barnet County Court to request a further 28-day extension to be able to remain in the house.

In the meantime, he said he would do everything he could to find us local, suitable accommodation so that we could avoid being evicted from the house along with our furniture and belongings. While I was talking to that gentleman, I was shaking like a leaf on a stormy night. I drove to the local court on Friday to complete and submit the request form for the extension that I was entitled to.

On Monday morning, I took my son to school, then went to court to appear in front of the judge to explain why we needed a 28-day extension to remain in the house. At that meeting, I was accompanied by my mother-in-law's other son. My brother-in-law told the judge about his mother's disability and what a negative impact it would have on her and my young son if we were sent to an unsuitable accommodation orout of the catchment area. He also explained that my son was going through a lot of stress and he must not be uprooted from his friends as it would have a severe impact on him. At that meeting, the housing representative officer was also present.

The judge understood our needs and permitted us to remain in the matrimonial home for a further 28 days but was very firm with our housing representative officer. The judge explained to him that he would not grant any further extensions whether we had suitable accommodation or not and told him that it was the local housing department's responsibility to help our family find appropriate accommodation.

Life is a Gamble

Two weeks after the court hearing, I received a phone call from the housing officer. The former officer was replaced with a woman who told me that they had found a temporary accommodation on the ground floor. It was a two-bedroom apartment in Barnet at the end of a council estate. She wanted me to go to see it the following morning.

'How long is the apartment available for, 'I asked her.

She replied, 'I don't know. The old lady who lives there is very ill in hospital at the moment. I don't know how long she will stay there. We have stored her furniture and all her belongings, and you will need to do the same while we are looking to re-house you into a permanent accommodation. You can bring all of your family belongings but no furniture.'

I still had no job, the father of my child had not supported us financially since he left (nearly eight months), and my mother-in-law had no money.

'Oh dear,' I said to the housing officer, 'I have no money to pay for storage, and it will break our hearts to leave furniture behind in the house. This is all I have left my life, and I can't afford to replace it.'

'I understand, Dee, but the rules are the rules.'

'Yes, I suppose they are. 'It was so difficult to feel gratitude facing such profound loss. But I was grateful for the work these people did to find us suitable housing during this desperate time.

That whole situation was like watching a tragic movie with a plot too complicated to follow. The only thing that I was sure of was that there were no guarantees – I had to be ready for anything. It was exhausting.

Just as I was getting used to the idea of leaving my furniture behind, the housing officer called again later that day for a different reason.

'Good news, Dee! The temporary accommodation I offered you this morning is now available as permanent.'

'What? How is this possible?'

Her voice lost some of her enthusiasm when she answered. 'Well, our office received a call from the lady's family to say that, unfortunately, she passed away this morning. So, it's good news for you, but sad news for their family.'

About the same time that my housing situation was in such a state of flux, my younger brother, Radovan, arrived in the UK. He married an English woman by the name of Caroline. From the moment he arrived in the country, he became my moral support and helped me navigate my new life, especially when I felt so ill-equipped to handle practical things like home repair.

After I got the call about the permanent accommodation, I took my son to school as usual. For moral support, I invited Radovan and Caroline to come with me to meet the housing officer and view the flat. When we entered the flat, it reminded me ofa neglected nursing home: dirty, dilapidated, stale-smelling, depressing. The kitchen had an ancient cooker and one cupboard on the wall. The carpet was torn and lifted off the floor. Walking on it was unsafe. The bathroom smelled of incontinence. It was tiny and not suitable for my disabled mother-in-law.

While the housing officer was showing us around, I cried, thinking I would have to reject this flat. If I only had myself to consider, I could deal with it as I came from an impoverished background. But I had to consider David and my mum-in-law. *This is the place I will be bringing the two people that I most love. How can we go from a five-bedroom house with all the luxuries to this hovel?* My mum-in-law would have to share a bedroom with me. As irrational as it was, I feared seeing her artificial leg. The flat was too small and would take a sizable financial investment I didn't have to make it habitable. *I have to tell her this won't do, either.*

As I was looking round the place with a sour expression on my face and wiping tears that wouldn't stop spilling from my eyes, I told her, 'This is not at all what I expected. This place is horrible.'

'Dee, no accommodation that we can provide will be ideal. You have to accept what we are offering and be willing to compromise.'

'Compromise? I can compromise. I promise you that! But please, put yourself in our position. Would you move your family into somewhere like this?'

The housing officer's reply was, 'Mrs S, this is the best accommodation you will ever get. I promise you.'

I couldn't believe what I heard. The flat reminded me more of Serbia than anything I had seen in England. My other question to her was, 'If this is the best, what is the worst then?'

'Much, much worse,' she said.

We were lucky to have the support of my brother and sister-in-law. Radovan took me to one side and said, 'If it's true what the lady is saying, then we suggest you accept this flat. I'll bring everything from the house and refit it in this place. I'll dismantle the kitchen and bedroom furniture and refit it all here. Don't forget everything that you have in the house is all yours and new. You only lived there less than a year. 'He continued, 'By the time I finish, you'll have a fitted kitchen, bedrooms, bathroom and a new carpet. Don't worry. I'll bring everything from the house and refit it all here. Then I'll decorate for you. It's going to look beautiful, Dragica, I promise you.'

Radovan and Caroline gave me the reassurance and support (both moral and physical) I needed to move forward with my new life, such as it was. If it weren't for them, I would have struggled for a long time. But thanks to both of them, my stress was tremendously reduced.

I looked at the apartment in a new light. My generous brother would help with renovations. It was on the ground floor and wheelchair friendly. There would be no burden of mortgage repayment hovering over my head like a storm cloud. The flat was in the same catchment area so that David could remain in his school.

I accepted the offer.

The next day, I took my mother-in-law to see it. I was worried about her reaction. I told her in advance that we were required to share one of the bedrooms because of a housing authority rule (two people of the same sex were expected to share except in cases of married couples). She was concerned about her privacy and my uneasiness about her artificial limb. She also had other health issues making the small space untenable. As I feared, she hated the apartment.

What I didn't know was that, while we were waiting to be re housed, my mother in-law's family helped her buy a two-bedroom place for herself near her original flat (where she used to live before she moved in with us). She said, 'Darling, you need not worry any longer about me moving with you or moving three of us together at all.'

It was a pleasant surprise under the circumstances, and I was happy and relieved for us both.

'However,' she said, 'I am willing to take the risk for my grandson and you. I will keep my name on the list until you and my grandson move in there.'

She was sensible and helpful. If she hadn't kept her name on the list with us, God knows where we would have ended up. They would have placed us with other young, displaced families in housing plagued with drugs, alcohol and violence. Instead, we remained on a list sensitive to the needs of the infirmed and elderly – a much safer housing option for all of us.

Thanks to Mum's family, she was able to buy another flat. Although I was not happy to be separated from her, my son and I were able to move into the flat in our own bedrooms that my brother had promised to decorate and do whatever needed to be done for us to make it liveable.

When we left the house, my son and I moved into the flat with no cooking facilities or sleeping arrangements. My brother Radovan worked round the clock to make the place as lovely and well-designed as possible. When he'd finished all the work, the apartment looked beautiful. David and I were comfortable and loved living there. During that time, my son stayed on and off with my brother and sister-in-law and their baby daughter. They lived in a generous, one-bedroom flat and shared facilities with four other tenants while they were waiting to be re-housed themselves.

Radovan and Caroline were so excited and happy for us to be moving into our own accommodation without having to share other facilities with other tenants. From their point of view, we were the lucky ones. What they failed to understand was that we had just left luxury accommodations to move into a slum-like flat, and, for my son, it was further away from his friends and his school. We did not feel quite so fortunate.

I was raised in poverty, so the step backwards was not as jarring as it was for David, who only knew a life of relative privilege. He always had new toys, designer clothes and a beautiful house to live in. When he was eleven all of that had changed. His dad had left the matrimonial home, and all the luxury went out of the window. Yet material wealth did not mean as much to him as the two of us being together and staying together.

I will always remember what my darling son said to me. 'Mum, if we have to eat baked beans on toast every day, I don't mind as long as we're together. That's all I care about.'

What must have been going through my sweet child's head? Probably that his dad had left him, and he didn't want his mum to do the same. What insecurity he must have felt at the time! I stood by him as long as he needed me and I always will be there for him no matter what. My son is my world, and he will always be a special person in my heart.

When we left the house, my son was upset. For my sake, he tried not to show it. I was heartbroken for him, but for his sake, I, too, kept my head up high.

I told him, 'We're going to be all right, David. We'll be happy again.'

He nodded, a shaky smile gracing his angelic face.

We hugged each other for a long moment.

Unlike his father, I was not lying to him. I just didn't know yet how I would make my promise to him come true.

Life is a Gamble

Chapter 19

Finding My Way Back to Me Again

During that troubled time, I kept beating myself up asking why I'd given Mike so many chances in the past, hoping he would change but knowing somewhere deep inside that he wouldn't (or couldn't). Why couldn't I accept that he never cared one bit about anyone else but himself – probably not even the woman that he left us for without any financial support? All of my regrets, guilt, and self-reproach created a dismal atmosphere round me. It was not healthy. It was not *me*.

I refused to fall into depression. Mike had poisoned too much of my life while he was in it; why should I let him continue to bring me down now that I was finally rid of him? I needed a plan to process my feelings, not ignore them, so that I could deal with them and let them go.

Each morning after I took my son to school, instead of going home or to a friend's flat for a chat, I drove to the local cemetery. I walked round for hours reading headstone inscriptions from loved ones. I cried while reading and would get more upset when I read messages for young people and children. One might think that I was crazy or morbid, but I wasn't. I was just trying to work out my emotions in a private, safe space.

I'd sit down by the graves to read the messages. Often, I'd cry my heart out. I felt so sad and alone. I was not crying for the dead people, as I didn't know them. I was crying for myself. I needed to release my frustration, sadness and anger with what was going on in my life. The cemetery was my confessional.

I was also telling myself, *you have a wonderful and healthy son. He didn't ask to be born. He's innocent in all this, and he needs you. And you need to look after him. He needs you. He needs you. He needs you....* The more I said those words, the quicker I started to think differently. My problems weren't permanent; they were temporary, an inconvenience that needed to be sorted out. I told myself, *you can do it. You are the only one who can do it. In the end, you will all be fine.* From then on, I kept repeating those words every day and used them as an affirmation. I started to feel better, stronger, more like *me*.

Regardless of how odd my coping strategy might seem, my solitary time at the cemetery each day for many weeks worked for me. I knew that the cemetery was the only place where I felt safe and peaceful, where I could be myself with no one to criticise, bully or harass me. No one would shout at me for saying or feeling the 'wrong' thing. The cemetery was not a morose or melancholy place; it was my sanctuary.

I tried telling my friends about how I felt, but they were often more interested in telling me about how I *should* feel or what I *should* do. Very rarely would anyone merely listen to me. The last thing I needed was to be judged, no matter how well-meaning the advice. I needed a place where *my* voice could resurface and be heard. For that, I needed silence.

During my cemetery visits, I found my own answers. They felt good and right and true. Solitude doesn't work for everyone. Cemeteries are not comforting for everyone. I'm merely saying that I was fortunate to find a way to coax my true self out of hiding in the shadows after so many years of confusion and fear.

After a little while, I invited a long-standing friend for coffee in my new place that was still not quite sorted out. During her short visit, she had so many questions and suggestions about what I could have done differently in the flat and my life as a whole.

'Thank you for your suggestions, but I've done a lot of thinking and sorting myself out already. I spend many lovely hours in a local cemetery just dealing with the feelings that come up. It's been helpful. I feel so much better about everything. I even have some ideas for the future – all from my quiet time in the cemetery. 'I smiled at her.

She frowned at me. 'Do you pay respects to anyone in particular?'

'No. I just wander round reading various headstone inscriptions. At first, they would all make me cry. Some still do, but some make me smile. And sometimes I just sit and think.'

She leaned back in her chair as if trying to create a safer distance between her and me. 'Why on earth would you visit a cemetery if you don't know anyone buried there?'

I tilted my head and pinched my eyebrows together. 'I just explained that.'

She tugged at her skirt and smoothed out her napkin, avoiding eye contact. 'It's very peculiar. 'She then cleared her throat. 'I don't mean to get too personal, but did you have some sort of...of breakdown? What medication were you on at the time? That could explain all of this.'

I was deeply offended. But I didn't want to lash out or offend her, so in a calm and composed manner, I replied, 'I never had a breakdown, nor did I take any medication before, during or after my marriage ended. My parents taught me to be strong and to cope with whatever is thrown at me. That's exactly what I did. Remembering my parent's advice is the only medication I'll ever need.'

'But, a cemetery? I don't think that's healthy for you. Isn't that depressing?'

'No, it's quiet so you can hear your thoughts. And there's no one to judge you like you're judging me now.'

Her voice rose in both pitch and volume when she said, 'Look here! I'm not ju –'

I interrupted her. The time for diplomacy was over. 'Yes, you are judging me! I'm glad you weren't round when I was having all of my troubles. Could you please finish your coffee and leave? And please, don't contact me again. 'I went into my bedroom until I heard the front door open and close.

She called again, but I refused to talk to her as that was not the first time she had been a negative and unsupportive friend. Eventually, she understood where I was coming from and decided to respect my wishes. I never saw her again. I believe good friends can be life preservers buoying you up through turbulent seas; bad friends can be anchors.

Even today when I have any worries, I visit my in-laws' graves (sadly, my mother-in-law passed away in 1994). They were two people that I had great respect and love for. When I need to talk to someone in confidence, I speak with them. I have not taken any antidepressant tablets before, during or after any of my problems. I'm proud of myself for that.

From then on, my positive thinking helped me to stay sane. I learned how not to be defeated by every small or large setback. Instead, I learned how to rally every time I was feeling down about the past or present. That's what I did then and what I have been doing up to now. It was a good feeling to be able to cope with any problem that was thrown at me.

My life has never been easy for me, but those times of housing and financial insecurity were tough. One problem I never had to deal with, though, was worrying about David. Rather than becoming angry or trying to escape his pain in drugs or other ways, he remained positive and supportive. His mantra was, 'As long as we're together, Mum, we'll be okay. 'Through all the emotional upheavals and being jettisoned out of the safe, secure, comfortable home and lifestyle that money temporarily bought us, David carried on. He focused on the future and what we had, not the past and what we lost. And what we had was an unbreakable bond.

My son, my best friend, my inspiration, my David.

He went on to graduate and attended Sussex University where he earned a Bachelor of Science degree in Chemistry and then a Master of Science degree in Technology and Innovation Management (with distinction). He devoted his career to working on global climate change policy projects. My darling son is my biggest inspiration to me and always will be. He gave me a reason to carry on living when life seemed hopeless. I wanted to make him as proud of his Mum as I was of him.

***

Once I felt better about myself, I had to formulate a plan for the future. Our security depended on having enough money to be independent. We were struggling because I wasn't working at the time. When we moved into the flat, I went to a local job centre to sign on and get some financial help until I found full-time employment.

When I arrived at the job centre, there were a couple of men and one woman drinking cider out of bottles outside the building. It was at 11am.These people already looked drunk. The waiting room was full of people, but they were shrouded in a hazeof cigarette smoke (the ban on smoking in public buildings hadn't been instituted yet). People were shouting: 'I need money for food!' 'My kids are starving!' 'I'm not leaving till I get the money I deserve!'

I was shocked as I had not seen or heard anything like it before. I scanned the room and walked out. I said out loud, 'Get out of here, I'm better than this. 'Then I thought, *come on, you can do better. Get a temporary job to put food on the table for you and your child until you find a full-time job.*

And that's what I did.

I didn't want to be like those people that live from day to day waiting for government aide. I always found work and made the best of it. My parents always said when I was growing up that the best help I could get was when I helped myself and worked hard.

The job I found was cleaning private houses. I did that while looking for full-time employment. I had self-respect, confidence, enthusiasm and enough drive to go back to work and succeed in life. That attitude helped me find a great job that used the skills developed in my former housekeeping career in a setting more closely aligned with my dream career: nursing.

I applied for the Area Domestic Manager position in the Estates and Facilities Department which provided all non-therapeutic services to NHS Foundation Trust mental health facilities (for example, maintenance, catering, cleaning, security, grounds keeping, and parking). In this position, I would be responsible for managing the cleaning standards of eight to nine different healthcare sites, including large psychiatric hospitals, administration departments, various clinics and doctor surgeries.

I was interviewed by the Estates Operational Manager and the Clinical Manager. Amongst other questions, one question that stuck in my mind even today was, 'Dee, what can you bring from the hotel experience that will benefit us?'

My answer was clear and confident. 'I will bring good customer service and good cleaning standards. I assure you that I will do my best to deliver. This is not just lip service. If you give me a chance, I will prove to you how good a job I can do for you.'

What a cheek on my part! But it worked.

The same day, at around 5pm, I received a phone call from the Operational Manager, to whom I would be reporting. She said, 'We are pleased to offer you the position of Area Domestic Manager. We would like you to start next Monday. Is that possible?'

'Yes! And thank you!'

I cannot tell you how excited and happy I was. This would be my first full-time job in a long while. I kept thinking, *I will be able to support myself and my young son financially and be able to pay the bills without having to worry any more.* I was a single mother who did not need government assistance. To start a new job gave me self-esteem. Even though I didn't have a chance to fulfil my dream of becoming a nurse, at least in a different way, I would be able to help patients by providing a sanitary environment and proper cleaning standards. I was just buzzing with excitement, and I couldn't wait to tell David the good news. When I did, he was thrilled for me, too.

My life, at last, seemed to be on the right track. It felt as if nothing could stop me from smiling. Then, out of nowhere, something did.

Life is a Gamble

Chapter 20

Crash! Bang! Bad News

I tried to contact my family as much as I could, but it was difficult. They didn't have a telephone for the first five years that I was away. I had to make advance arrangements with their neighbour who had a phone. So, my calls were regular but infrequent. I wanted to call to tell them the wonderful news about my new job.

The same Monday evening I was offered the job as Area Domestic Manager, I spoke with my middle brother, Dragan. He was a police officer and the one who gave me all the advice about how to stay safe and look after myself in the UK before I left Serbia. We spoke for quite a while about many things. He seemed genuinely happy about my news and that my life was headed in a good direction.

Then he spoke with my son. They were laughing and joking as usual; they were very close. They said goodbye to each other, and my brother requested to talk with me again.

'Dragica, I would like to come over to the UK to see David and you again. Soon.'

'We would love that, Dragan! Just let me know when and which airport you'll be arriving at. We'll wait for you and pick you up.'

He said, 'Okay, I will. 'My brother sounded his usual, happy self.

That was the last time we spoke to each other. I never saw him alive again.

Two days later, on a Wednesday morning in 1994, my sister-in-law, Caroline, was visiting me with her two young children. David, who was sixteen, was at college. The house phone rang. I picked it up.

'Hello?'

My nephew, who was also sixteen, said, 'It's me, Auntie. Uncle Dragan has had an accident. He died.'

'What are you talking about? What kind of joke is this?' I knew no one in my family would ever make a joke like this, but I couldn't yet comprehend the idea that my dear, happy brother was dead.

My nephew said, 'I'm sorry, but he has committed suicide.'

The phone went dead.

I stared at the receiver for a moment then gently placed in its cradle. Then I started trembling uncontrollably.

Caroline came over to me and grabbed me by the shoulders. She asked, 'What is it? Tell me what's happened. You're scaring me!'

I looked at her, but the words got stuck in my throat. When I closed my eyes, I found my voice. 'Dragan is…is dead. They say he…he ki…killed him…himself. 'I pressed my palms into my face as if closing my eyes and covering my face would make the reality of his death go away. Of course, it didn't.

From left to right: my youngest brother, Radovan (who was married to Caroline), my oldest brother, Zivoslav, and my middle brother, Dragan.

My sister-in-law and I hugged each other. I kept saying to Caroline, 'Please just tell me this is not true. What is wrong with my nephew to joke with something as serious as this? No, it can't be. We spoke to my brother two nights ago, and he was happy. He said was coming over to see us.'

My sister-in-law was incredibly supportive of me, but it was hard for her, too. We were all close as a family. I lost a brother; she lost a brother-in-law. We both cried, but I was inconsolable with grief.

My sister in-in-law suggested that I call my parents' house. 'Please brace yourself –Srecko wouldn't be joking with something like this. Go on, call them. I'm here for you.'

I will never forget that phone call. As soon as someone picked up the phone over there, I could hear my poor mother and sister wailing for my dead brother. I heard many other voices in the background comforting and looking after my family. To listen to them in that awful state broke me into even more pieces. I felt helpless.

I couldn't say anything else to the person who answered the phone other than, 'This is Dragica, we are coming to Serbia. 'I put the phone down.

Through all that confusion and sorrow, I thought of my brother in England and my son who had already left for school that morning and just missed that fateful call from my nephew to tell us about my beloved brother's premature and tragic death.

Oh, my God, I thought, *how can I break the news to my son who is very close to my brother and is looking forward to seeing his favourite uncle soon?* How could I break the news to my other brother? I simply felt numb.

My sister-in-law took charge. After a little while, she said, 'First things first, we need to go to my house and tell Radovan,' meaning her husband. 'Then you two go to college this afternoon to pick up David and bring him home. Then tell him.' That was suspect in itself as I didn't usually pick my son up unless we had made prior arrangements.

When we got to their house, my brother opened the door to our forlorn faces – the kind of expressions that come with bad news.

He took a deep breath and asked, 'Okay. Who died, Mum or Dad?'

I mumbled as I cried and said to him, 'Oh, God I wish it was both of them instead. 'I just stared at Radovan. I couldn't speak anymore. My jaw was locked. I was in shock. I couldn't even cry, so Caroline had the burden of telling him.

My brother was devastated. This was the first close death in our tightly-knit family. Dragan was only 42. We were both in tatters thinking not just about the brother who we adored and lost but how we lost him. We thought about our poor parents and the rest of the siblings. How were they coping without our support? None of us expected that any of our siblings would pass away before our parents, but it happened. The grief was unimaginable.

We needed to sort out our plane tickets to leave the next day to travel to Serbia to attend my brother's funeral. I will always give my sister-in-law credit. She is more like a sister to me. She was and still is my rock. Caroline was amazingly supportive of all three of us. I gave her my credit card, and she booked two return tickets to Romania, as in 1994 there were no direct flights to Belgrade due to United Nations flight suspensions before the country was bombed.

All these arrangements had been made, but David still was unaware that his uncle Dragan was dead. After his last lesson at college, my brother and I went to pick up my son. I took David to Serbia ever since he was a baby. As he was growing up, he loved the country life, and he loved my family. They loved him, too. David was especially close to Dragan as he lived in Belgrade, 200kmfrom my parents, and would always wait for us at the airport. We spent time with him, and he would take my son around Belgrade. My brother was a police officer and would take David to the police station before we went to see my parents and rest of the family. Every time we visited Dragan, David was always fascinated with Serbian police uniform as it was different from the English police uniform. From a very young age, David loved putting my brother's police uniform on. Dragan would take cartridges out of his gun – the very weapon he eventually would use to take his own life – then he would let David hold that gun. David would shout with pride, 'I'm a policeman!' As he was saying this, my brother would melt with pride. As he didn't have any children, he adored my son, my nieces and nephew.

My son was proud of my brother. David loved Dragan and everything about him. For this reason, it was excruciating for me to break the news to him that his favourite uncle had committed suicide.

David saw us in the school car park with our pitiful faces. I could not contain my sorrow and started to cry, and he just knew something terrible had happened. When we told him in the car that someone had died bizarrely, he asked the same question as my brother, 'Who is it? Granddad or Grandma?' As he was so close to all my family, he didn't want to hear that any of them had gone.

I plucked up the courage to tell him, 'Sorry, my darling, it's your favourite uncle that is not with us anymore. Uncle Dragan is dead.'

The silence was sickening.

'David, I have booked tickets for your uncle and me to go to Uncle Dragan's funeral.'

David was shattered. He got out of the car, leaned on the car door and just wept. Then he just stopped (I assume because he was in shock), turned to me and said, 'Mum, what are you talking about? Uncle Dragan is dead? Dead how?'

I was trying to stay strong for him. As calmly and tenderly as I could, I explained, 'He killed himself with his own gun. As you know, police in Serbia carry guns with them at all times. They even bring them home. That's the system over there. He took his own life with the same gun he carried for his job.'

David just hung his head and shook it as if saying, *no, this can't be true.*

'Listen to me David, darling. I've booked tickets for Uncle Radovan and me to leave tomorrow for Uncle Dragan's funeral. 'I had my hand gently resting on his back.

David looked up at me with both sorrow and astonishment contorting his face. 'Mum, what do you mean two of you are going to my uncle's funeral? What about me? I want to go and see my uncle for the last time. I need to say goodbye to him. Can you please get me a ticket? I want to come with you two.'

'You're right, darling. What was I thinking? Of course, you should come with us. 'I hugged him.

In the midst of his sobs, I heard, 'Thanks, Mum.'

The next day, the three of us travelled to Romania by plane and then on a private minibus to Belgrade. When we arrived outside my brother's apartment, there were no lights inside, so we presumed that our dead brother's body had been taken to my parents' house 200km southwest from Belgrade where the funeral would be held the next day. We decided to continue our already lengthy journey to my parents' house. I just wanted us to get there as soon as possible, but it felt as if we had been travelling forever.

We arrived at my parents' house in the early morning. Much to our surprise, we learned from my distraught, inconsolable mother that Dragan was still in Belgrade's hospital mortuary. She told us that Dad was so upset that he had gotten on a coach and travelled three hours to Dragan's apartment in Belgrade, hoping to see his son before they moved him to the mortuary. When Dad got there,my brother had already been taken away. As this was a suicide, my father was not able to see his son in the mortuary immediately. I can only imagine how hard it was for my dad not to be able to see his own child. Instead, he went back to my brother's apartment with the intention of supporting Svetlana, his daughter-in-law, but she ended up consoling him. The poor woman had enough worries without having to tend to her father-in-law, too. Unfortunately, Dad was overwhelmed by sorrow and was not fit to care for himself. He became very ill. Mum also told us that Dad had been anticipating our arrival in Belgrade last night. He had wanted all of us to travel together with my brother's body back to our birthplace.

I immediately called Dragan's house to talk to Dad. Overcome with grief and lack of sleep, my father was devastated and angry with us. When I told him our decision to travel home after not seeing any lights at Dragan's house, he scolded me. 'How could you do it? Your brother's nails have not gone blue yet, and you didn't stop and come in. Shame on you both. 'There was no mercy in his raised voice.

All I said to him was, 'Sorry dad. We are coming.'

I was concerned about him and his state of mind. He needed us now more than ever. He needed our support. As soon as I got off the phone, I said to my brother, Radovan, 'We need to go back to Belgrade. Straightaway. Dad needs us.'

Radovan nodded.

I left my son with the family. Radovan and I went back to Belgrade.

When we arrived, my dad looked decrepit: unshaven and curled up in the corner of the bathroom. There were lit candles placed on the edges of the bath where my brother had blown his brain up with the gun that he used to use for his work.

My dad was visibly relieved to see us. He reached out to us while repeating, 'Why? Why? Why?'

We all cried.

I wished I could answer my father, but I, too, only had questions. *What drove Dragan to do it? How could he take his own life? How could he be so selfish?* I felt that he was punishing us all. *Why? Why? We all loved you, and you loved us, didn't you? You seemed happy when I spoke to you a couple of days ago. Were you planning on killing yourself then? Why didn't you tell me? Could I have done something to stop you?'* Unfortunately, there were no answers, or the answers went away with him.

My dead brother's wife, Svetlana, managed to give my dad medication. We persuaded him to have some soup. Eventually, he came round, thank God. Around lunchtime, we left Belgrade with my brother's body. We followed the police van that took my brother back to his parents' home. He was buried the same day.

It is heart-wrenching to lose someone as close as a brother, sister, mum, or dad, but it's torturous to lose your own child as my parents did. Many parents who have lost and buried a child understand. I listened to my parents crying and wailing, calling my dead brother's name as if he might come back if only they called loudly enough. I thought my heart would break.

In Serbia, the coffin lid is left open until the burial, giving the family and close friends a final chance to say a proper goodbye. I couldn't do it. *I am not saying goodbye to my much-loved brother.* I put one hand under Dragan's head and another round his body. *I won't let you go!* How could I let go of someone who was my brother, my inspiration, and my advisor, who told me how to look after myself and stay safe when I arrived in the UK many years ago? It took my family some time to get me off my brother's body to let him rest in peace.

When I stood up from his coffin, I was numb. I went into total shock when I saw my right hand covered with blood from his wounded head. The next thing I remember, I was laying on the lawn next to my brother's grave. I was told that I fainted and didn't want to leave until he was properly buried with all the flowers and wreaths placed on top of his grave.

My dead brother will always be close to my heart until we meet one day again. It has been 21 years since that tragedy happened, but it feels as if it was yesterday. People tell you time is a great healer. It's true. But individual strength and personal choice guide each person through their own bereavement path. I have healed as much as I could, but I always think of Dragan and my poor parents (who are no longer with us). I feel that my parents grieved so much for my brother that they went to their early graves heartbroken. As a result, each time I think of one of them, I think of all of them.

But life continues regardless of the tragedies that befall us. I had a new job waiting for me back in the UK and a son who needed his mother's love and attention. I would need every bit strength and determination I could muster to create the personal and professional life I wanted. But would it ever be enough?

Chapter 21

My Experience Working for the NHS

Three days after my brother's funeral, we returned to the UK. I called my new employer. She was pleased to hear from me, and we agreed that I would start my new job the following Monday. I was well-supported by both staff and management, especially by the Operational Manager who had interviewed me and given me the job. At the time, she was my line manager and couldn't do enough for me.

She took me to two of the largest hospitals to introduce me to my new staff then left me with them so that we could become acquainted with one another. After introductions were made all around, I gave them some background on me and my approach to work. I told them, 'I haven't worked for the NHS before, but I'm looking forward to working with all of you. I see this job like any job: as a challenge. If we work together, we will provide a good cleaning standard for the patients. That's our goal.'

I looked at the sea of faces that represented my large staff. Some were smiling and nodding, others looked sceptical, and still others had blank expressions. My

English was fine, so I knew they understood me. The only explanation for their mixed reaction, then, must have been that I was very different from their former manager. I was positive and enthusiastic while setting out clear expectations for standards of excellence. NHS staff in that hospital seemed laid back and did as little as possible. They weren't used to having a manager like me who had worked in four and five-star hotels and was eager to bring those high-quality services in the hospitals as I had promised at the interview.

As an Area Cleaning Manager, I was responsible for managing cleaning standards for eight to nine different NHS sites. I was taken round to be introduced to site managers and domestic staff I would be managing. It took every bit of professionalism in me not to show my disgust at how dirty and neglected these sites were. Even more disheartening for me was the fact that my new line manager, who was taking me round those sites, was the person managing them before I was employed.

I questioned how my supervisor who left these places in such a dismal state could possible evaluate my work? I couldn't help myself. I asked him why those hospitals were so dirty.

He shrugged his shoulders and said, 'I was always short of staff and couldn't achieve the good cleaning standards that were expected of me. That's why we employed you, Dee. We're hoping you will do better.'

I chose to take his answer as a compliment, but I was gravely concerned about the level of dirt and risk of infection in those hospitals for the patients and staff. *How could any domestic manager allow this to happen? How did he get away with it and not lose his job?*

A few weeks on the job solved these mysteries for me. Cleaners and supervisors were not trained how to do their jobs. During my early days, I witnessed how permanent staff were lazy and treated reporting for work as optional. But even when absent, they still got paid. I couldn't understand why this was allowed to happen. My predecessor said he was short of staff most of the time, but 50 percent of his full contingent of staff were not turning up for work on a regular basis.

Supervisors would call the local employment agency for back up. Their staff would turn up without any training in cleaning protocols, and they were not familiar with the unique requirements of hospital sanitation. As a result, minimal proper cleaning was done, and the agency charged a great deal of money for casual workers who were paid more than the permanent staff.

Agency cleaners would use one damp cloth for dusting all day; sometimes it would be rinsed between rooms, sometimes not. The permanent staff were just as bad. The same buckets and mops were used with the same water to mop a whole ward with twelve to thirteen rooms, plus offices and a food storage pantry. At the end of the shift, the mop and the water in the bucket were equally filthy and foul-smelling.

I was horrified at what I witnessed in the early days of my employment. Many things had to change…and fast.

In the 1980s and 90s, patients were still allowed to smoke in the wards, even in mental health hospitals. With smoking comes ashes, discarded butts, nicotine-stained surfaces and other cleaning challenges. Some psychiatric patients were too ill to know where they were. They urinated in the dormitory, on toilet floors and in corridors. The two large hospitals I was managing (and many others) were both disgusting and not fit for purpose. But 'my' hospitals were no worse or better than other mental health hospitals I visited in the London area. They all suffered from the same problems. But there had to be a solution as the current conditions seemed inhumane.

When I asked the nurses why they weren't complaining about their dirty wards, the answer was always the same: we do, but no one cares. Their response saddened me. Patients were forced to live in (and staff was working in) a filthy and unhealthy environment because no one bothered to clean it up.

I promised them that I would do everything in my power to improve cleaning standards as soon as possible. With time, we did just that. We did it as a team. I began by creating a schedule to clean the wards more frequently than in the past. Training was next. I implemented training records and trained the supervisors on how to check the cleanliness of the hospital. Instituted weekly meetings with nursing staff as they were able to help by supervising clients. Getting the nurses to join our efforts was easy once I reminded them that we had the same goal: to improve the health of the clients by keeping the hospitals clean and providing a good environment.

A couple of months into my new employment, two domestic cleaners were signing out to go home at the end of their shift. One of them said, 'We would like to confess something to you, Dee.'

'What is it?' I asked. 'Tell me please.'

They were both foreign and outspoken. The Italian domestic asked her Greek colleague, 'Niki, what do you think about our new manager, Dee?'

Niki's answer was, 'Well, she comes across as a Hitler. Do this! Do that! Or it's off to the Gulag for you!' She was mocking a stiff-limbed military officer.

I had to admit, it was funny. I laughed. But I listened, too. 'So, Tina, is that how you feel?'

She replied, 'No, you are nothing like Hitler! What you are teaching us makes sense. I think you are going to be good for us. Maybe the bad workers should worry, but you will look after the good workers. That's what I told, Niki. 'She was blushing.

I couldn't argue. That's what I had said to them, and most of the staff agreed with me.

Tina said, 'This is what we want to tell you. We like you. We will support you all the way.'

I was so pleased to hear that. 'Thank you. I'll definitely work with you all and give you the support that you all deserve.'

Implementing change is never easy, but the rewards were slowly manifesting. We were headed in the right direction, and I felt good about my accomplishments. My supervising line manager went on long-term sick leave due to a nervous breakdown. He did not come back to work. The woman who hired me started supervising me again. This manager put all her trust in me, giving me complete freedom to do my job the way I thought was best. I loved the faith she had in me. In the meantime, she was advertising for a domestic manager who would become my line manager.

I worked for the NHS for about a year before my new line manager was hired and something positive started to happen. In October 1998, I was talking to Heracles, who was married to my friend, a former Yugoslav woman by the name Blagorodna (Beba). He encouraged and helped me purchase my apartment that belonged to a local authority.

As soon as he started to explain, I lashed at him verbally and said, 'How can you even suggest this to me? My wages are only £13,000 a year. At the moment, I'm just about managing to pay the bills and put food on the table for my son and me. If anything goes wrong in or out of this apartment, all I need to do is call the council, and they will put it right, free of charge. But if I get a mortgage, I'll have to pay for everything myself and my mortgage will be more than I'm paying now in rent.'

Heracles listened patiently to what I had to say. He knew I was frightened about finances. But he never suffered fools gladly. He persisted, 'Don't be ridiculous, Dragica. Listen to me now, please. Yes, it's all easier now. But in the long run, you'll have nothing to show for yourself or your son. The first few months or first couple of years, it will be hard for you, but remember your wages in the NHS will go up a little every year, and you will catch up. Every year it will get easier.'

This is what I call a good friend. And a wise one.

He was right. I started with £13,000 a year, but within ten years of working for the NHS, I was earning £40,000+. With those wages, I was comfortably repaying the mortgage. In addition, I set up a private pension with the NHS. I contributed three percent of my wages each year for eighteen years until I retired in 2010.

Heracles also pointed out to me, 'When you decide to move from here, you can sell this property and use the profit to put down a good deposit for a new property in a better area and hopefully have money left over to help your son. You understand what I am saying to you, Dragica? Your son will need some help with university fees. Now, what do you say?'

I took a deep breath. I liked the idea even though I was worried about what I was about to do. I said, 'Heracles, you are absolutely right, but I am scared. I have no idea where to start.'

Heracles, a good friend of the family and the person who was instrumental in helping me to become independent.

'Whoa, whoa,' he said. 'Wait a minute. You have nothing to worry about. I will come with you to the Nationwide Building Society and support you all the way until you can stand on your own two feet and feel comfortable to manage on your own. 'What a good friend he was, still is and always will be.

A few days later, in October 1998, we both went to the building society and applied for the mortgage. It was granted to me. I bought our two-bedroom flat for £23,500. By then, my son and I had already lived there for six years and, being a council tenant, I was entitled to a discount. As a single parent and on low wages, I could not afford to buy the flat from the local authority for the next four years – until my wages were considerably increased. Also, if we stayed there for another four years, I would have been able to purchase that property from them for a 50 percent discount.

After I bought that little flat, I never imagined that one day I would sell it. I had experienced many losses in my life. This apartment represented something I did on my own with my courage and my initiative. It was David's and my home. I earned it, and no one would ever take it from us. My son and I settled in nicely, and by then we both felt safe. Heracles suggested that one day I should sell it and move from there. *No,* I thought, *I never want to uproot David again. He needs to know where home is. So do I.*

But I didn't expect what happened next.

***

In 1999, I started dating a lovely man, Dave, who I met through work. He worked as a Senior Electrical Engineer in charge of all the electrical suppliers for the hospital. We had a whirlwind romance and got engaged within a few months. Our lives changed forever and for the better. I adored Dave, and he got on well with my son. We were all happy. Unlike my ex-husband, I trusted Dave, and I truly loved him. I still do. He is the man of my dreams.

When I met Dave, my son, David, was already at university. After a year of being with Dave, we talked about selling properties – his house and my flat –then buying joint property for ourselves to live in. It seemed right. I remembered what Heracles suggested about making a profit on my property, so I agreed with Dave and sold the same apartment for £169,000, £145,500 in equity. I was able to help my son with his university fees and pay for half of the new house with then my fiancé, Dave. We have been living there ever since.

I will be thankful to Heracles for rest of my life for making my son's and my life easier financially and for helping us to have a more comfortable life than we would have had without his help and advice.

Change was all around me, but this time, the changes felt good. David was at university. Dave and I had a solid, loving relationship. Now I just had to get a new supervisor at work. I hoped that whoever it was would have the same vision as I did for excellence in cleaning standards and a firm but kind management style.

The job for a senior domestic manager was advertised, and I was looking forward to having a line manager again. This person who started to work with us was from another hospital where he was a clinical waste manager. This meant he had no experience in cleaning and was lacking in management skills. But the two of us got on very well.

Due to his lack of experience, he relied heavily on me. He knew I had long-standing experience from the four and five-star hotels. His strengths were managing clinical waste for all the sites and doing administrative work while I got on with the practical side of the job like training, checking cleaning standards, looking after the staff and customers, and hiring and disciplining staff (if and when required). Together we implemented staff training records such as colour coding on cleaning equipment, cloths, and mops and buckets to prevent cross infection. This type of coding did not exist prior to our efforts. Most of the time he stayed in the office being an administrator while I was continually going out on sites to educate supervisors on how to do their job and how to train their domestic staff to clean wards properly. Thus, we complemented each other.

Between the two of us, we provided a reasonably good cleaning environment for patients and staff, but it was challenging to keep the standard up as long as patients were allowed to smoke and urinate in the dorms. At the time, we were based in a hospital in North West London where I stayed and worked with my manager for eight years. Because of my hard work there, I was well-respected by management, staff, patients and customers. And I enjoyed my job tremendously. I felt as though I could do no wrong.

But an opportunity presented itself that seemed too tempting to turn down. A door opened. I walked through it. But the path on the other side was not what I expected.

Life is a Gamble

Chapter 22

Surprises of My Professional Success

In September 2003, NHS Foundation Trust was advertising for the position of Facilities Manager to start working in the old hospital for a six-month secondment and, within those six months, to take charge and move the patients and staff to a brand-new hospital nearby. I was well-known by the new management team as they were our customers when I worked as the Area Domestic Manager in the Estates and Facilities Department. I supervised all of their housekeeping.

I applied for the job, and an interview was arranged. On the same day of the interview, I received a call on my mobile from my new line manager before I had even reached my old office. She said, 'I am happy to offer you the position of Facilities Manager. I need you to start as soon as possible as I will be going on holiday soon. Please let me know when you can start.'

I was elated. This job offered more professional opportunities and a much better salary than my former job. However, I was anxious about breaking the news of my departure to my present manager and, more so, to the Associate Director. She had initially given me the job when I most needed it and supported me all the way up to that point. In a way, I felt I was letting her down by leaving.

I rallied my courage and told my manager, 'I have found a new job. I would like to go for a six-month secondment.'

He frowned and shook his head. 'Dee, I cannot let you go. I need you here. Letting you go would be detrimental to this department. It will have a negative impact on everyone here. Six months is too long.'

How selfish, I thought. *I supported you 100 percent, and this is how you are repaying me? This is not right! What do I do now?'*

With my manager's permission, I went to talk to the Associate Director, hoping she would understand and support me as she had always done. It was important that they release me so that my current job would be waiting for me in six months. To my shock and surprise, when I mentioned my intention, her face changed from welcoming to irate.

She leaned forward over her desk, narrowed her eyes, and spoke in a deliberate, stern tone. 'No Dee, we need you here, and we will not let you go. 'Then, with a raised voice, she said, 'Now, go back to work! And I don't want to hear anything more about this.'

She shouted at me as if I were a little girl, not one of her managers. I left her office crying for two reasons: the way she spoke to me shocked and demeaned me; and I had just learned that my dear sister, Milka (who had been so ill as a young girl) was gravely sick with pancreatic cancer. I wanted to go back to Serbia to support her through a potentially life-saving operation. With my bosses' attitudes, I doubted they would allow me to take time off again.

All I wanted from my manager was to be a little bit more supportive of me and give me her blessing to do as I wished. It was then that I realised I was a victim of my success. My bosses were bullying me to stay because I was effective at my job. But what gave them the right to hold me back from my family obligations or career aspirations? Nothing! I lived in a free country, and I was no one's caged bird.

After I left the Associate Director's office, I took a deep breath, wiped my tears away, and went to see my new potential manager to explain what was happening. I told her I might not be able to work with her temporarily after all.

This lovely woman with whom I worked happily for the next seven years, Kate, said, 'Dee, I want you here, and it's going to be for more than six months. That's all I can say. 'She nodded, smiled, and had sincerity in her eyes when she spoke with me.

We shook hands.

The next day, I handed my one-month notice to my current employer. My previous manager and his line manager called an urgent meeting with me. They tried very hard to keep me by offering me various courses, but not a better job or more money. Therefore, I politely turned their offer down and left.

A week before I was supposed to start my new job, my sister's health deteriorated. I felt pulled to be with Milka given the urgency of her condition, but I hadn't worked even one day at my new job. The stress of not being able to be in two places at once gnawed at me. It was an exhausting and punishing time.

I plucked up the courage and went to see Kate again. Before I could say anything, tears started rolling down my face.

'What's wrong, Dee?' She sat next to me.

I told her about my sister.

Her whole body softened. She spoke with such compassion, such kindness. 'I am sorry to hear that. Please go to Serbia to see your sister and stay there for a week. One week of you not being here won't make much of a difference to me, but it will make a big difference to you and your sister. Dee, just go.'

From left to right: my middle sister, Milka. me and older sister, Zivka,

I could barely utter, 'Thank you, Kate. Thank you so much.'

Kate said, 'When you come back, you will be able to concentrate on your job.'

I nodded, too filled with gratitude and relief to speak.

I was on a plane to Serbia the following day, anxious to see my sister. Milka had an operation that lasted hours. As soon as she was out of intensive care and stable, I came back to the UK and got on with work with my new staff and management.

That's when the troubles started with my previous employer.

I thought I was bullied in the past by my previous bosses in the hotels, but at least they were my direct supervisors. This time, my *previous* employer was bullying me.

My previous employer became my provider for all the services my new employer required. In effect, I went from providing services to the hospitals to working in the hospitals that relied upon the services that I used to deliver. Since I was now my former employer's customer, one might think they would have treated me with the deference or respect typical of any client/service provider relationship. This was not the case.

I left their employ without their 'permission. 'They were still upset with me, so they were unprofessional in our new relationship. They refused to cooperate with me but providing me with quality services to support the facilities was their job. They refused to cooperate with me for the first six months I was in my new position, making that trial period hellish for me. I wanted to prove that I could do an excellent job, but my service providers were blocking me at every turn.

When I started my new job, I tried to communicate in a civilised manner with my previous bosses and colleagues. In return, each department head was rude and obstructionist (except Dave, who was always sweet and discretely cooperative). I regularly faced arguments when I requested contractual services. I was told I would have to pay extra or special arrangements would need to be made for necessary, immediate services. I knew full well that what I was requesting was part of the standard contract, but these diversions slowed the process of getting my job done. They just did not want me to succeed.

As a facilities manager, I was responsible for all hospital services in a large hospital with nine wards. Part of my job was to have monthly meetings with my providers, who also happened to be my previous employer. At those meetings, my assistant took the minutes of the meeting, including the agreed-upon scope of services and summaries of pertinent discussions. But when the minutes were distributed to all attendees, the head of Estates and Facilities would ask for a copy and challenge various points in the minutes via terse emails or hostile phone calls to my office. That sort of behaviour was upsetting and frustrating and for me. Trying to resolve all of their supposed issues also wasted valuable time I could have spent doing something productive for my staff or the patients we all served.

Adding to my stress were personal concerns. My sister was still gravely ill. I worried about her incessantly. At the same time, I found out that my new love, Dave, had prostate cancer. A thick fog of anxiety seemed to have descended upon me, and the way out was obscured.

No matter how disturbed I was, I would tell only bits and pieces to my new line manager, Kate. I didn't want her to think that I couldn't manage my service provider or my personal life. Instead, I battled through and tried my best to persuade my former colleagues to cooperate for the good of the patients.

In June 2004, we moved into the new hospital. I needed to have reliable, professional services to run the facility; instead, I had a bunch of bullies from my former job who clung to their grudges against me and were willing to sacrifice patient safety and comfort for revenge. It was lunacy.

I realised that, after six months, I couldn't sort out this problem alone. The situation was getting worse rather than better. So, my director stepped in and stopped it all.

One morning, I was in the new hospital making tea for myself in the tea area. My director walked into make herself tea.

'How are you, Dee?' She smiled as she busied herself preparing her tea.

I smiled back at her. 'Do you really want to know or are you just being polite?'

She stopped what she was doing and looked at me. 'Of course, I do, Dee.'

'Then please give me five minutes in your office if you can…please?' I asked.

She gave me more time than I had asked for.

I told her that I loved my job, and I was happy with staff and management at the hospital, including my line manager, Kate. Then all of my troubles with the Estates and Facilities Department and my private concerns about Milka's and Dave's health came spilling out of me.

After I told her about all my problems, she rested her hand on mine and said, 'I am so sorry to hear about all the problems you are experiencing, Dee. I hope your sister and your Dave will fully recover. You're doing a good job here, Dee. As far as Estates and Facilities are concerned, leave it with me.'

I don't know what she said to the Estates and Facilities Associate Director, but within a week, everyone, including the Head of Estates, was fully cooperative. From then on, we all got on providing the service to our patients that they were entitled to. At last, I felt like a proper and respected customer of their services, not their disobedient ex-employee. This was all thanks to my professional and compassionate director.

Dave had his operation for prostate cancer and was recovering at the same time as my sister, but it was easier for me to cope with my private stress without having to go through the daily tension of battling with my service providers. Both my sister and my fiancé fully recovered from their operations. I continued to work happily at the same hospital for another six years, In May 2010, I retired healthy and happy.

Like so many people, my life has been a journey of twists and turns while cycling up and down a mountain range. Friends used to tell me not to give up, that life will get easier. I believed them because I have an optimistic, positive disposition (even after all the challenges I have faced both personally and professionally). But I couldn't help wondering, *when will my life get easier? When will it be my time to revel in happiness and contentment? When will most of my journey be a gentle downhill slope, wind to my back, with no sharp curves ahead to worry about?*

Meeting Dave, I thought, was the start of my easier journey. In many ways, it was. But there were still some hairpin curves and uphill climbs ahead for me.

Life is a Gamble

Chapter 23

Meeting the Love of My Life

It took me ten years after Mike left to trust another man. Then, I met Dave. I suppose I was finally ready to meet someone special and kind. And believe that his feelings were authentic. If Mike was my poison, Dave was my antidote.

We met in the hospital where we both worked, and it was love at first sight from my point of view.

I asked one of his colleagues, 'Is Dave married?'

His reply was honest and disappointing. 'Yes, he's married. 'Then he winked at me and said, 'But if you like him, he'll take you out, wine you and dine you. He's a good man.'

I frowned and crossed my arms. My reply was polite but infused with resentment. 'Please forget I asked. Let me tell you something. Someone had an affair with my ex-husband, and I'm very much against affairs.'

Dave and I had respect for each other, but he didn't know how I felt about him at the time. And I certainly wasn't going to let him know. Five years passed. Dave was still working in the same department. My feelings for him hadn't changed. It was agony seeing him every day and not being able to act on my feelings, but I had to be strong. He was married. End of story.

Unfortunately, Dave's wife had struggled with breast cancer for years. The cancer had returned in 1987. In 1999, she became very ill and, sadly, passed away. When I was told about her illness, I thought, *thank God I didn't cross that line. Otherwise, I would have taken the guilt to my grave about having an affair with a sick woman's husband.*

Dave is a private person, and not many colleagues knew about her illness until she was too ill and in and out of hospital. One morning a colleague of ours asked me, 'Dee, did you know that Dave's wife is very ill?'

'No,' I said. Even though we were friendly, Dave hadn't said anything to me about his wife's condition. I decided it would be best keep quiet and let him handle his personal affairs the way he always had: in private. After Dave's wife died, he took a one-week compassionate leave. Upon his return to work, I went to his office to offer him my condolences. 'If you need to talk to someone, I'm here for you.'

He gave me a sad smile, nodded and said, 'Thank you, Dee.'

I returned his sad smile and left his office.

After that, Dave and I often met during our lunch hour. Dave spoke about his late wife, how he really felt during her illness, and his what it was like being alone after 37 years of marriage. He also talked about struggles in life, something that we both had in common. I was able to understand and empathise with what he was going through fully. Sharing our grief and our life stories – good and bad – brought us closer together, but we continued to be platonic friends.

A few months later in that same year, I went on holiday to Cyprus. This was nineteen years ago. Dave gave me his home address so I could send him a postcard. I missed him the moment I left the UK. Dave told me (when I returned) that he had missed me, too. I sent him a postcard. One of the things I wrote on it was, 'The place is lovely, people are great, what else can I say, Dave, except I wish you were here?' As hints go, this one was rather obvious.

When I returned to work, we greeted each other at the reception area. Our daily lunchtime talks continued, but the content shifted from our problems to our feelings and current life situations.

After a few days, he said what I had been waiting years to hear. 'Dee, I care about you. I realised this when you went on holiday. I missed you very much.'

'That's nice,' I said, 'I missed you, too, Dave. *How romantic,* I thought.

When I met Dave, he was a shy and quiet person, but after we declared how we felt about each other, he plucked up the courage to call me at home. I found out later that he had taken my phone number from the management contact list.

When I got home, I was told by the young refugee woman who lived with me temporarily that 'someone had called. 'She was a young mother with two young children under five from war-torn Serbia who was on the waiting list to be re-housed with the local housing authority. I thought she was winding me up. Since I returned from holiday, I would bash her ears talking non-stop about Dave, so I wasn't surprised that she remembered his name.

The next day, I asked Dave, 'By any chance, did you call my home last night?'

He ran his hands through his hair then rubbed his neck. He was nervous…or embarrassed. 'Guilty! Yes, I did. But it was quite innocent, I assure you, Dee. I wanted to ask you if you would go out to dinner.'

'Really? You're not joking with me, are you?' I could feel my face blushing like a schoolgirl.

'No, I'm quite serious. What about Saturday?' he said. His eyes gently captured mine.

I couldn't stop gazing into his soft, kind, beautiful eyes. With a trembling whisper, I replied, 'Yes, that would be nice. Thank you. 'I was so much in love.

On Friday night, I was working late. There was a knock on my office door. It was Dave. I invited him in. As it was after five pm, the evening domestic staff was cleaning the main office next to mine. My office was so small that it could only fit my desk, a filing cabinet and two chairs. Dave and I had no choice but to sit close to each other. Our knees were almost touching, and I think we were both embarrassed by it. I was 50 and Dave was 59, but we both felt like two lovebirds in our twenties, thoroughly besotted with each other. Never having had a proper boyfriend in my life, the feelings that Dave stirred in me by his mere proximity were new, exciting, strange, wonderful, and confusing.

'We're still on for dinner tomorrow evening, right?' Dave's face was a combination of hopefulness and trepidation. His face was aglow as if the office was too warm. It wasn't. He must have felt awkward, but he maintained proper eye contact.

I became so shy and embarrassed that I kept flicking my long blond hair away from my face and looked everywhere but at him. I finally answered him, 'Yes, of course. But I would prefer that, instead of dinner, we just go for a drink. Would that be all right?' I didn't want to offend him, but I had only spent short bits of time talking with him. A dinner date seemed so *serious*. Yes, I was love struck by this man. But what if our date didn't work out? Just drinks seemed less formal, shorter, and easier to exit gracefully. I suppose my experience with men over the course of my life had left me wary.

We arranged to meet the next evening half-way between his place and mine. From there, we would go to the pub I had chosen. Back then, there were no mobile phones; instead, people used pagers. On my way to meet Dave, I received a message on my pager that there was an accident on the road, and he would be a little late. There was not much I could do but wait. As the evening was rather cold, I sheltered myself on the step of a closed pub. Dave passed me by without either of us noticing. He returned down the Dartmouth Hill looking for me. I called his name. He jumped. I could see the relief on his face. He was happy I hadn't stood him up.

When I saw him, I was gobsmacked. Dave was so well groomed, his hair distinguished, grey and shiny. His shoes were so well polished that you could almost see the stars overhead reflecting on them. As we were walking hand in hand downhill towards his car, my legs were unsteady. I felt as I was walking on shifting sands.

My heart was pounding. I was in heaven. I felt like the happiest person on the planet. When we got in his car, Dave presented me with a long, slim, green box and said to me with a tender, loving voice, 'This is for you, Dee.'

I was so nervous that I couldn't open it without his help. I felt like an idiot. A single red rose lay in the box. I still have the rose today, fifteen years later. I directed him to a pub near where I used to live in High Barnet, North London. We sat down to have a drink.

Dave just kept looking at me in an adoring way.

I was waiting for him to say something, but nothing came forth. It was both comical and a bit uncomfortable. I shifted in my seat and excused myself to use the loo.

When I returned to the table, Dave said, 'I'm sorry. I'm not a conversationalist. 'He made a small shoulder shrug. 'I don't know what to say.'

To put him at ease, I said, 'Never mind, Dave. Let's talk about work, something we are both familiar with. How was your day today?' I asked.

His face melted with relief. He released a big breath he must have been holding in from the start and said, 'That's good, thank you.'

Within half an hour we had both relaxed enough to feel ourselves. He put his hands over mine. We talked about all manner of topics for hours, continuing to hold each other's hands and looking into each other's eyes. Both of us were utterly love-struck. From that moment, we knew that we were meant for each other and that our lives would be spent together.

'Dave, it's getting late. Would you like to come to my place for a coffee?' I tipped my head and gave him a small smile.

He returned a bright, enthusiastic smile, saying, 'Yes, please. I would love to.'

'Okay,' I said. 'Would you like to follow me?'

'I'd love to. Thank you,' he said.

We both stood up.

I turned around, looked at him, and said, 'Bloody fool, you'll live to regret this for the rest of your life.'

'I don't mind. Why not die happy? He winked at me.

I called Bettie, my temporary Serbian refugee roommate, to say that I was bringing Dave back for coffee. While I called her as a courtesy, I was hoping that she might take it upon herself to tidy the place up a bit. Since her arrival with her children, my apartment looked as if a bomb had hit it. Toys, clothes, and food seemed to be scattered hither and yon. Anything of mine that was tasteful or decorative had to be removed from the reach of the children.

But the night I brought Dave home, my flat was transformed. I could smell a mixture of something delicious baking and furniture polish when we arrived at around 10:30 pm. Bettie told me that she was more or less sure I would invite Dave back for a coffee. She didn't want to let me down by bringing him to messy place and not having anything to offer him apart from tea or coffee. I was so proud of and grateful to Bettie.

When we got in, the children were in bed sleeping, and the whole flat was spotlessly clean. All of my personal items were back in their original place (after three months in hiding). As soon as we sat down, she offered us tea and coffee. In the blink of an eye, she came out of the kitchen carrying a tray with tea for two and banana cake that she had made during the evening while the children were in bed.

Bettie was ever so supportive of me as far as Dave was concerned. Her wish was for me to be happy again. She sat down with us to chat. I acted as the translator for them.

Fifteen minutes later, she told me in Serbian, 'Stop kicking me under the table! I will leave shortly. 'She rolled her eyes at me.

I began to laugh.

'What did she say, Dee? Let me in on the joke!' Dave was laughing even though he didn't know what was happening.

I told him what Bettie had said.

'Oh. 'Dave's chuckles ebbed as he cleared his throat. It seemed as if he didn't know what to do or say next, so he kept quiet and focused on his tea.

Bettie took this as her cue to exit. She went to bed.

Dave and I spent the next few hours together in my living room. Talking. Just before the end of the night we both declared our love for each other and agreed that we wanted to spend the rest of our lives together.

'Have we both lost our minds? Acting like young lovebirds?' I asked Dave as I nuzzled into his shoulder.

'I'd say we're acting like mature lovebirds. And if this is losing our minds, it's quite a lovely feeling, don't you think?' He drew me even closer to him.

I just sighed with contentment.

The next day, Sunday, I spoke to Bettie regarding her housing problem. 'Enough is enough. Bettie, you have been with me for three months already. If I don't put my foot down with the homeless department, you'll be more or less in the same situation as I was ten years ago, which means you can end up anywhere.'

'Have I done something wrong, Dee?' Bettie's voice quivered.

'Oh, please don't think that. No! You and your children have been wonderful. It's just time that you find a place of your own and start your new life here. I'll go with you tomorrow to the housing department to help sort things out. 'It was true; I wanted her to start a new life in her own home. It was also true that I wanted my flat to myself because Dave had become an integral part of my life.

I went with Bettie and the children to Barnet Housing Department the next day and demanded they find her suitable accommodation as soon as possible. The very next day, I received a phone call from Bettie's housing officer to tell me that they had found temporary accommodation for her and her two children not too far from where I lived so that we could visit each other.

I called Bettie to tell her the good news. We were both happy and anxious for her to make the move as soon as possible (but for different reasons). I was at work and had already taken time off the previous day, so I could not take her to the housing department to pick up the keys to her new accommodation. Instead, I called one of my friends from former Yugoslavia who became a good friend with Bettie, too. She was more than happy to assist Bettie with all the necessary arrangements. They accomplished their mission, and we had dinner together when I got home. Then I took Bettie and her children to their new accommodation.

Bettie moved out of my flat with the children on Monday and Dave moved in with me on Wednesday of the same week. I hadn't planned on things moving so quickly with him, but I didn't mind, either.

I was at work that Wednesday. At the end of my shift, I got into my car to go home. Unfortunately, my car wouldn't start. I called Dave to assist me. He did. When the car started, he sat in the passenger seat. We talked for a few minutes then I started the engine and was ready to go.

'Thank you, Dave! What would I do without you? Well, I guess I'll see you tomorrow.'

'Oh no, not tomorrow. I'm coming with you now,' he said. He wasn't joking. He came with me and never moved out. So much for me promising to myself that no man would move into my flat because of my bad experience with my first marriage. I thought I would never trust any man with my heart and wellbeing or David's security again. I'm glad I was willing to take a chance on Dave.

My home was my security, but my Dave was my destiny. I shouldn't have painted every man with the same brush coloured with memories of Mike.

Four years later, Dave and I sold our properties, and from the profit, I made after selling the flat I was able to pay off my son's university fees and give him some financial help to get on the property ladder as Heracles Economides had suggested. The rest of the money from my flat and the proceeds from the sale of Dave's house went into buying a beautiful bungalow for cash. Dave and I love our little home. For me, it represents the kind of comfort and security I longed for (but never had) during and after my failed marriage. That it took so long in coming only makes me savour its sweetness more.

I've learned many lessons as I've grown older. An important one is to embrace opportunities when they appear rather than shrink from them. I could have remained suspicious of all men, never giving Dave a chance. Instead, I opened my heart and gambled on him and me. I grabbed the opportunity for happiness with both hands. And I have no regrets.

Out of my first marriage came a magnificent, caring and loving son, so I do not regret that, either. David, my son, means everything to me. My two David's have admiration, respect, and fondness for each other. I'm overjoyed that I created and sustained a loving, supportive family unit, even if it took me most of my life to do it.

I would need the support of my loved ones because there were still more challenges ahead of me.

Life is a Gamble

Chapter24

Brotherly Love

Health is a time bomb that could explode in anyone and at any time.

My older brother, Zivoslav, lived in Russia for 30years. I couldn't afford to visit him over there,so we always met in Serbia at our parents' house with our other siblings.

The last time I saw my brother was in 2010 in Serbia. Most of our family, including Zivoslav and me, caught a virus lasting for 48 hours. Zivoslav had to go to Belgrade to sort out some documents that he needed to take with him back to Russia.

As he had to wait 48 hours for the paperwork, he decided to visit our older sister, Zivka, who lived some 80 km away from Belgrade. Traveling did not help his condition. When he returned to our parents' house, he looked exhausted, pale and gaunt. We were all concerned about him.

'How are you feeling?' I asked him.

'Oh, not too bad. I probably have what you all have, a virus. 'He told us not to worry; he would be okay.

I was worried about him going back to Russia as ill as he was and urged him to go to see a doctor. He promised me he would. Then we went our separate ways – him home to Russia and me home to the UK.

I called him to find out if he went to see the doctor and how he got on.

'Well, doctors over here think I have Tuberculosis [TB].'He tried to keep his tone light, but his cough told me he was still sick.

'TB? Zivoslav! That sounds bad.'

'Dragica, you worry too much. The medication they gave me is working. Forget how I sound. I'm feeling better.'

'Really?'

'Yes, really. Try not to worry. They said after three months of treatment I'll be as good as new. I'll even be able to go back to work.'

'That's wonderful news! Aren't you happy I told you to see a doctor, Zivoslav?'

'Yes, Dragica, you're a good sister. Bossy, but good!'

In October 2010, I sent him some money to help him out a little. I knew something wasn't right when the money that I sent to him wasn't picked up from Western Union. Since they had no house telephone where they were living, I couldn't call his wife, Katia, and ask about my brother's health or why the money that I sent in Zivoslav's name hadn't been picked up. I would find out later that, by then, he was in and out of hospital. He didn't want me to worry, so he didn't tell me that he was hospitalised.

By December, I had a gut feeling that my brother was deliberately keeping secrets from me regarding his health – and the secret he was keeping was not good. I kept calling him on his mobile, and he kept telling me, 'Relax. Stop worrying. I'm getting better.'

But I knew him better than he knew himself. We were only one year apart in age, and we grew up together. I felt very close to my brother. As much as I wanted him to let me into his life regardless of how painful the reality might be, he wanted to protect me from the truth of his condition.

I relaxed for a while but didn't stop calling him to check in on him. In March 2011, I told Zivoslav that I was coming to Russia to visit him. He panicked. I thought his reaction was odd until he asked me to wait to visit until after he was clear of TB. Since TB is highly infectious, I understood and honoured his request. I insisted, however, that he give me Katia's mobile number. After my constant pestering, he gave me her number.

I called her. Unfortunately, Katia spoke very little Serbian, so I could barely understand her. 'Zivoslav in hospital. 'That was all I could decipher.

If I wanted more details, they would have to come from my brother.

In mid-May 2011, my brother finally told me something of substance. 'Dragica, they found something inside my chest that needs to be removed.'

'What is it? How will they remove it?' A hundred more questions were swimming in my mind.

'No one knows what it is…yet. Doctors want to treat me with antibiotics. If that doesn't clear it up, they'll operate to remove it.'

'Oh, dear. 'I didn't want to say what I was thinking: *please, God, don't let be cancer.*

'Don't worry,' he said. 'I'll be all right.'

At the beginning of June, my brother told me that he was going to another hospital to see a specialist and would have an operation to remove the growth from his chest. The specialist, an oncologist, did a biopsy. The news was as bad as it could be. The oncologist told Katia that my brother had cancer, and it had spread all over his body. He had only two-to-three months to live. Zivoslav was only 63years old. For all these months, the doctors had been treating him for TB because they misdiagnosed him. In that time, this aggressive form of cancer spread. Fast. Had they diagnosed him accurately in the first place, there is a good chance my brother would be alive today.

Katia sent me a text after the oncologist spoke to her, but I couldn't understand it as it was in Russian. But the mere fact that she sent the text told me that she wanted me to know something important.

I desperately needed to get to Russia and get there fast. But it wasn't going to be easy. I didn't know their home address in Sochi. I had only seen my sister-in-law once in 20 years back in Serbia, so I wasn't sure what she looked like. My brother could have been in any number of hospitals, but I couldn't find out which one without knowing how to speak Russian. And I still had no idea what Katia's text said. It could have told me that he was cleared of TB and perfectly healthy! I needed to know the content of that text before deciding to go there.

I panicked and imagined the worst about my brother's health. In desperation, I stopped people on the street and visited pubs, health centres and schools to ask if anyone could help me with Russian translation. It was useless. Feeling helpless and frantic, I visualised the sand in an hourglass steadily pouring from the top to the bottom; when all the granules had fallen, my brother's life would be over. I had to see him before that happened.

On the way home from North London, I decided to visit a small local shop. I politely asked with my voice trembling, 'Is there anyone who can speak Russian, please?'

To my surprise, the shop owner, Mustafa, answered. 'I can speak Russian. Can I help?'

I burst into tears and couldn't talk for a moment. Then I said, 'Thank you, God, thank you for helping me find this wonderful man!' I explained the situation to Mustafa, and then asked him, 'Would you mind speaking to my sister-in-law, Katia, on my behalf?'

'Oh, yes! Of course. Anything to help.'

I wanted to hug him. After I dialled Katia's mobile number in Sochi from my mobile, I handed it over to Mustafa. 'Please ask exactly what is happening with my brother's health and why that hospital sent my brother back to Sochi without operating on him.'

He nodded and started speaking in Russian.

While he was listening to her, a sad expression clouded his face. The news he heard from Katia was bad. I just didn't know how bad.

He put his hand on the phone mouthpiece, then he said to me, 'I am sorry.'

I wiped tears from my eyes and face. 'No. Please tell me whatever it is. I need to know.'

'Your sister-in-law told me to tell you that your brother, Zivoslav, has an aggressive type of cancer and it has spread all over his body. He has two-to-four months to live.'

I began sobbing. Devastated, I kept saying to myself, *why, why, how? Four months ago, he was fine.*

I asked Mustafa, 'Please tell Katia that I will get the visa as soon as possible and travel to Sochi. I need her to wait for me at the Sochi airport to take me back to their place.'

He nodded and translated. 'Katia says she wants you to come and will meet you at the airport if you text her the date and time.'

As he handed my mobile back to me, I said, 'Thank you so much for your help and kindness.'

A few days later, I was on the plane from Heathrow airport to Sochi. This was in June 2011.

My Dave was sympathetic and reassuring at this disheartening time, but my family and friends were concerned about me going alone to Russia. I didn't know where brother's home was, or the hospital's address and I couldn't speak any Russian. The trip would be gruelling for me on many levels, so I, too, was concerned about my journey. But I didn't want anyone to know that I had even a moment's hesitation. My love for my brother was strong enough that no one was able to stop me from travelling to Russia.

On the day I was leaving for Russia, my Dave came with me to see me off at Heathrow airport. Dave made the poster with Katia's and my name on it, so when I got there, we could identify each other easier.

All the way to Moscow, I cried on and off and kept wondering why my brother didn't go to a specialist earlier. If he had, he would have had a greater likelihood of survival.

Life is a Gamble

In Moscow, I needed to change planes to a short internal flight to Sochi. I boarded the smaller plane, took my seat, got emotional again and started to cry. Two Bulgarian gentlemen were seated next to me. One of them spoke good English and, when he saw how distressed I was, asked me what was wrong. I told him about my brother and why I was travelling to see him. I also explained, 'I'm supposed to meet my sister-in-law in Sochi, but she only speaks Russian, and I don't speak any Russian. If for some reason, she isn't there, I have no idea what hospital my brother is in or even where they live. Then what will I do?'

'Ah, yes, I understand your concern.'

'Something very similar happened to me a long time ago. I was just 20 years old travelling from Yugoslavia to the UK without speaking any English. Arrangements were made for someone to meet me, but no one was there at the airport. And here I am doing the same thing 40 years later. 'I sniffled. 'I just want to help my brother in any way that I can.'

The gentleman that spoke English warned me. 'Please, if you get to Sochi and your sister-in-law is not waiting for you, don't get into any taxi by yourself. It isn't always safe.

Russian drivers are okay, but there a lot of Kurdish minicabs drivers who are dishonest or even dangerous if they think you are vulnerable. Just be careful. 'His advice was beneficial, but he also put fear in my head.

I decided that I wouldn't trust anyone I didn't know (unlike my naïve trust in Nada and John who conspired to assault me when I first came to the UK). If Katia was not at the airport, I would go to the police and ask them to help me find my brother in one of the two hospitals in Sochi. It wasn't a great plan, but it seemed like a safe one.

The closer we got to Sochi, the more anxiety I felt about being stranded at the airport and having to fend for myself. I kept praying, *please, God, let Katia be waiting for me when I come out of passport control.*

The Hungarian man noticed my escalating agitation and made me a very generous offer. 'I can see you are nervous. I would like to stay with you at the airport to make sure you meet your sister-in-law or get to some safe accommodation. At the very least, I can be a translator for you.'

'Oh, my, that is so kind of you! Are you sure you have the time?'

'Of course, I do. I am happy to help.'

A part of me was suspicious of this stranger offering to help me, but I knew I would need a translator whether Katia met me or not. 'Thank you, Sir. You are very kind. 'I gave him a wobbly smile.

As I was coming through the airport, I held the little banner with Katia's and my name on it. Then I heard a distressed voice calling my Serbian name, 'Dragica, Dragica.'

As soon as I heard my name being called, I immediately felt a sense of relief. Katia was waiting for me! While embracing each other, we both cried and cried.

The Hungarian gentleman waited for us to greet each other. As he promised, he translated for me what Katia was saying. She told him to tell me that she was so happy that I arrived to be there for my brother when he needed me most. She also told him that Zivoslav knew that I was coming, and he was looking forward to seeing me. Again, we embraced each other as tears flowed freely down our faces. Then, we both thanked the kind Hungarian gentleman for being such a gracious translator.

As it was just before midnight when I arrived in Sochi, it was not possible for me to visit my brother in the hospital that night.

I was taken by Katia and Dime, her son from her first marriage, to their holiday home where they lived with my brother. On the way there, I had many questions about my brother's health, but due to the language barrier, answers would have to wait until I saw my brother in hospital the next day. I couldn't wait to see him, put my comforting arms round him and let him know how much rest of the family and I loved him.

I was also hoping to find out from him, what had already been done, what more could be done for him at that hospital and how I could help financially (or in any other way). That night, I hardly slept. Early the next morning, Katia and I got on the coach and travelled an hour to the hospital to visit my brother. The rush hour traffic was horrendous. My brother kept calling Katia from his mobile, eager to find out when we might arrive. I, too, was impatient and grew even more so as we inched along in the heavy traffic. I just wanted to get there.

Finally, the hospital came into view. From a distance, it looked well-maintained. *At least my brother isn't in some dumpy, neglected place,* I thought.

As we entered the hospital grounds, Katia shouted, 'Dragica! Dragica!'and pointed her finger towards the hospital entrance. Then she said, 'Zivoslav!'

I got unnerved because I had no idea what she was going on about. Then I understood. She had spotted my brother alone in a wheelchair outside at the front entrance of the hospital. From what I had gathered after the phone call Mustafa had translated for me, my brother was frail and virtually bedbound. So, why was he outside and unsupervised? How did he even manage it?

Katia continued to call his name as we approached him. He didn't respond. His chin was resting on his chest. He appeared both exhausted and confused.

Zivoslav and me in 2010.

While I was troubled about the state my brother was in, I was also infuriated at the lack of supervision by the hospital staff entrusted to care for him. What if my brother attempted to leave the hospital grounds and got on the busy main road? What if an unscrupulous person saw an opportunity to harm a defenceless victim? The temperature outside was 26.7 C. How long had he been out there in that hot weather? When we got to him, he was dehydrated, confused and he hardly recognised me. *What kind of hospital is this,* I thought.

I gave him a cuddle. When he heard my voice, my brother responded with moans of delight. He nuzzled his face against mine. He probably felt safer and happier because I was there. At least I hope so. I certainly felt better being there to care for him and advocate for him.

I was heartbroken to see my brother in that state. Only eight months ago when he was in Serbia, he looked well and looked his age– 63 – but sitting in that wheelchair, he looked 30 years older. He was unshaven, wore ragged clothes and he drifted in and out of lucidity. I was distraught seeing my brother in that physical and mental state. He was so ill. So frail. So vulnerable.

When we took him back to the ward on the seventh floor, we wanted answers from the nursing staff about how he managed to find a wheelchair, sit in it and leave the ward unnoticed. How did he get in the lift? How did he manage to pass by the security staff guarding the front entrance to prevent the very thing my brother did?

The nurse that my sister-in-law spoke to was not interested in being interrogated by visitors. Katia was confronting her because she knew the language. The nurse's face was red and pinched in a most disagreeable expression. She continued to put her hand nearly in Katia's face, finger pointed. Katia finally huffed, turned round and said in broken Serbian, 'Him room back to.'

I could see how distressed she was. I was troubled, too. I deduced that the nurse didn't offer any explanations or apologies. She just ordered us to take Zivoslav back to his room. When we entered my brother's room, I was horrified at what I saw. The bedding was filthy. The room was messy and unorganised. The walls were grimy. There was only one bed cabinet and one chair per patient, and they were dusty and dirty. And the floor was tacky and smelt of urine.

The other patient was about my brother's age, and he was as confused as my brother was. They both looked under-nourished. While I sat on the chair next to my brother, the other gentleman kept getting in and out of his bed. He was wearing only a t-shirt. As he wandered in and out of the room, he babbled to himself while urinating all over the floor. My sister-in-law called the nurse to attend to the mess. One of them came in the room with a dirty cloth in her hands, threw it on the floor, got hold of this old and sick patient and pushed him on to his bed while shouting at him. I couldn't understand what she was saying, but I could understand the tone: exasperation mixed with intimidation. I'm sure it's easier on the staff if patients are compliant, but the lack of respect or compassion was shocking to me.

The next thing that happened appalled me (both personally and professionally). This nurse stepped on the dirty cloth and pushed it round the floor with her foot to sop up the urine. Because she never rinsed it, she effectively just smeared it round the floor. When she finished, she picked up that cloth with her bare hands and took it away. I knew proper cleaning standards and patient services in hospitals (at least in the UK). Witnessing all this, I felt sick to my stomach that those patients were deprived of basic care, dignity and hygiene. I felt sorry for the rest of patients, my brother, and the staff. The entire hospital was dirty and putrid.

When the hospital cleaner delivered lunch, she left the plate of food on top of the dirty and dusty bed cabinet. His meal was a piece of uncooked chicken breast and one blob of mash potato. While Katia tried to feed Zivoslav, I fed the other elderly, sick and confused gentleman in the same room. He was so hungry that he ate it all, unlike my brother.

What upset me the most was that the cleaner responsible for cleaning patients' bedrooms and corridors did not wear protective clothing (i.e. uniform or gloves). All the windows were locked for safety reasons at all times, which made safety sense. But I saw no areas where patients had access to fresh, clean, outside air. As a result, the halls and patient rooms smelled stagnant and like urinals all the time. *How,* I wondered, *would anyone get better in such an unsanitary environment with little or no genuine care?*

I visited my brother in that hospital on Saturday and Sunday. That was enough to assure me I needed to intervene in some way to improve the conditions and quality of his care. Even if he couldn't be saved, he shouldn't have to spend the end of his life in such squalor. And if there was a chance that his life could be prolonged, it certainly wouldn't happen in that hospital. I couldn't wait until Monday to go back to the hospital with Katia. I started putting pressure on her for us to see the oncologist so I could ask my questions, hoping that I would be able to help my brother's current health situation in some way.

I found the name of one of my brother's Serbian friends, Ivan, in Zivoslav's mobile phone. I told him how appalled I was by the unsanitary environment and substandard level of care I had witnessed. 'I wouldn't put a dog in this kind environment, let alone a human being!' I also shared with him my concern for my brother's failing health. 'I must help him, but I need a translator. Will you do this for me? For Zivoslav?'

Ivan was happy to come to the hospital to help with translating.

On Monday, we scheduled an appointment with the oncologist. Zivoslav, Katia, Ivan and I waited for over three hours to see him. My brother was in constant pain. There was nothing I could do for him.

Ivan was getting bored sitting around, so he decided to pop out for a quick cigarette. 'If the doctor comes, just call me on my mobile, and I'll get back,' he said.

As soon as he left the building, the doctor came in and called Zivoslav and Katia to go with him to his office so he could talk to her in private regarding my brother condition.

I called Ivan. 'Come back to the ward straightaway. He's here.'

'I'm on my way.'

A few moments later, my mobile rang. It was Ivan. 'Security won't let me through. They say visiting hours are over. I tried to explain, but they won't listen.'

Damn, I said to myself, *why did I allow him to leave before we saw the oncologist?* 'Okay, Ivan. I'll try to see what I can do up here on my own. But could you stay…just in case?' I was frantic that Ivan wasn't with me when I needed him to translate what oncologist had to say about my brother's illness or to ask my much-needed questions through him.

'Of course.'

Katia followed the oncologist to his office. I kept saying, *'Interpreter please, Katia.* 'She could not understand what I was saying to her, and neither was she interested in what I had to say at the time. Understandably, she was worried about her husband and needed to see this doctor herself.

In a frustrated and abrupt manner, she said to me something about explaining to Ivan later and having him tell me all about my brother's condition. At least this is what I thought I understood.

Absolutely not! I thought. *He's your husband, but he was my brother first.*

I followed her and my brother's doctor to his office. Clutching my hands together, I waited for him to finish talking to my sister-in-law. Then I knelt down and pleaded with him to speak to me through the interpreter.

The oncologist took the report from the other hospital where my brother was diagnosed with cancer and given three months to live. With an angry face, he mumbled something and started to walk in front of me towards the lift. I realised that he was going down to find Ivan. I nervously followed him outside the building.

Ivan came over to greet the doctor and translate for me.

Before I even had a chance to ask the doctor anything about my brother's health, he abruptly asked Ivan, 'What more does she needs to know? Her brother has full-blown cancer. It has spread all over his body. There is nothing his sister or anyone can do for him to change that.'

What upset me the most was that he didn't show any compassion towards me as a relative of a sick patient. He acted as if I was wasting his time.

His brusque demeanour didn't stop me from asking the questions I had come all this way to have answered. Ivan translated his answers while my steady streams of tears needed no interpretation.

When I had no more questions, the oncologist said, 'If there are no more questions, then I must return to my work. 'Off he went. No handshakes. No goodbyes or well wishes. No human compassion.

I put my arms round Ivan and sobbed inconsolably for a few minutes. After I stopped crying, we both went back to my brother's room. We found Katia crying. She told Ivan to tell me that she was sorry for snapping at me earlier. I accepted her apology. She then told Ivan, 'I have made a decision after speaking with the doctor. As soon as I sort out his medications and release papers, I am taking him home. Tell her.'

'Home?' I was stunned. 'How are you going to cope with him in the middle of nowhere with no sanitary facilities? Your home is lovely, but it hasn't been properly finished yet. Toilet outside at the end of the garden. The kitchen is downstairs, and your washing facilities are at the back of the house. You don't even have a bath or shower yet, do you?' I must have had a wild-eyed look.

Katia lifted her chin, squared her shoulders and assumed a defiant but even tone of voice when she told Ivan to tell me, 'Zivoslav can still walk a little, and the weather is good. I will look after him properly at home. He is *my* husband, and he will be much better than here.'

And that was that. Within an hour, we left the hospital with my brother.

On the way home, Katia seemed to relax. Everything about her was much softer when she explained, 'The journey from home to the hospital is one hour and a half each day, and I am not well myself. I won't be able to visit him every day. If he stayed in hospital without proper care, food and regular drinks, he will die sooner, and I am not having it. It would not be fair to my husband to continue to stay there any longer.'

I had to agree with her decision when she explained it to me. And, after all, she was his wife. Whatever she decided was how it was going to be.

We took him home on 21June 2011. My brother was in excruciating pain even though he was given a generous dose of morphine. Even then, he couldn't sleep and kept wandering out of the house in confusion. He didn't know where he was and couldn't tell day from the night. Katia and I stayed awake and kept bringing him back, but he was confused and wanted to leave the house.

He repeated, 'I am going to find the doctor for myself. No one here cares about me. Nobody is doing anything about my pain, and no one is telling me what is wrong with me. I will go and find a private doctor to look after me and remove the growth from my chest. 'It got so bad that none of us could sleep during the night. As the two of us were worried about him escaping, Katia decided to put a padlock on the gate to prevent him from leaving the house unnoticed.

One of the hardest parts of caring for my brother was not being honest with him about his illness. Doctors in Russia have a policy to let family members tell patients that they are terminally ill. They believe a devastating prognosis often leads to suicide, and doctors want to avoid being blamed for any dire consequences. Thus, they leave it to family members to break the tragic news. Katia had decided not to tell Zivoslav, fearing he would kill himself to avoid prolonged suffering. I had to respect her wishes.

Yet my brother would constantly demand to know what was wrong with him. Was it kinder to lie to him or would the most loving thing have been to be honest with him? I still don't know.

The situation with my brother and his wife was quite grim. His health was failing, and she had her own health challenges. Their home, while private and comforting in some ways, was not an ideal place for two older people, especially one with terminal cancer. Added to my concerns about them was something calling my heart back to the UK. Dave and I had set a date in August for our wedding long before I knew my brother was gravely ill. I didn't want to leave Zivoslav and Katia in their time of crisis; but I longed to be with the love of my life, planning our wedding and focusing on happier thoughts.

I found Ivan's phone number and asked him to come to my brother's house. He came immediately. I think we were both desperate to help Zivoslav in any way that we could. Through him, I was able to reassure Katia that I was there for both of them. Whatever she decided, I would stand by her and be with her all the way. My sister-in-law was heartbroken about her dying husband; she was sorry for herself, too. As she was talking, tears were coming down her face as fast as snowflakes in a blizzard. We both cried in each other's arms while my brother was weeping and wailing in pain in the next room.

Katia took a deep breath, she wiped tears from her face and stopped crying. She became chillingly calm and quiet. An odd, vacant look replaced her normally expressive eyes. She turned around, looked at me, and fell into my arms. She kept talking in Russian, and I couldn't understand what she was saying. Then she said one word in Serbian to Ivan: *'kazi.'* *'Kazi '*means 'tell,' so when she said, 'Kazi Dragica,' I knew she wanted Ivan to tell me something. What worried me is the way she told him. Katia had pinched lips, furrowed brows, and was flushed. To me, she looked angry.

I panicked for a moment, wondering what awful thing she was about to reveal. Then I asked Ivan, 'Please tell me what she was saying. 'I'd rather know what I was dealing with than let my imagination run wild.

Ivan said to me, 'Dragica, Katia is in shock, she doesn't know what to do for the best with your brother. 'Katia continued speaking Russian and Ivan translated. 'I love your brother. Being married to him for the last 20 years, it is my duty to look after him. He is my husband

and, as you know, when two people get married, it is supposed to be for better or worse. I would like to do just that, but I am not able to do it due to my own illness. Zivoslav's illness is terminal, but no one knows how long he is going to live. As I said, I am unwell myself. After you leave in the next five days, we will both go under very quickly. I am scared, Dragica.'

I grasped both of her hands in mine, hoping my compassionate gesture would ease her pain. Her fear.

Katia continued, 'What I am about to say will be the biggest and most painful decision I will have to make right now, but I am ready for it.'

I felt as if my blood was draining out of me, dreading what she might say.

She didn't make me wait long to find out. 'Please call Srecko [his son] to come and take his father back to Serbia to look after him, so Zivoslav can spend what little time that he has left with his son and his young grandchildren. Dragica, it was Zivoslav's wish that when the time comes, he be sent back to Serbia to be buried next to his and your brother as well as your parents.'

After hearing Ivan's translation, tears welled up in my eyes. Katia and I gazed at each other through blurry eyes then hugged each other tightly. Our hearts were able to say what our words never could: *thank you for taking care of my beloved Zivoslav.*

I turned to Ivan, wiping my eyes and said, 'Okay.

'Although I could not imagine letting my terribly ill husband go to spend the remainder of his life without me, I was relieved that Katia had that kind of love and strength.

'Tell Katia that if it's my brother's wish to be buried over there, he should be transported to Serbia as soon as possible. Tell her we'll take good care of him…and…thank her for being such a loving wife.'

Katia nodded and tried to smile.

As I was already there, it made sense that I didn't go back to the UK (even though I had a return ticket to London). Instead, I decided to take my brother back to Serbia.

The very next day, I van accompanied me to the bank and to a travel agent to book the tickets for the following day. He also took me to the hospital to arrange private ambulance with a nurse to take us all (Zivoslav, Katia, Ivan and me) to the airport. Ivan wasn't only a good friend to my brother, he stood by me through a very difficult and stressful time in my life.

On the way to the airport, my sister-in-law was crying discreetly. My eyes remained dry. It's not that I wasn't feeling anything. Quite the opposite – I was a jumble of emotions. I was heartbroken that my dear brother was dying. But bringing him back 'home' to Serbia to be with his son and grandchildren and the rest of our family gave me such solace. Also, visiting his gravesite would be much easier in Serbia…when the time came. I would like to think that I controlled my tears and emotions during that ride to the airport for my brother and his wife. Separating after a long, loving marriage under these circumstances must have been torturous, especially knowing they would never see each other again. I had to stay strong for both of them. After all, I had an important job to do: to take care of my beloved brother. I had to put my emotions aside for the time being and show Katia and Zivoslav that I had my wits about me.

When we got to the Sochi airport, the nurse administered the last injection of morphine to my brother before we left. Airline staff took charge of my brother by putting him in a wheelchair. As we only had hand luggage, all we needed to do was to go through the passport control.

I will never forget my brother's and Katia's goodbye; it was heart-wrenching. They were both sobbing. Katia reached for my brother's frail hands and face, caressing him and saying a last goodbye to her beloved husband. Then she gently put her arms round him and wouldn't let go. She wailed like a lost, frightened child. Suddenly, she started talking in Serbian, using the few words she must have learned from my brother. 'I love you. I love you, Zivoslav, and I will always love you.'

At that point, I started to sob, too.

She kissed him on his forehead and said to him, 'Goodbye, my love. Until we see each other again... 'Then she let go.

We made our way toward the departure area. I heard Katia calling his name. She kept waving her hands in the air and calling his name until she couldn't see us anymore. I felt so badly for Katia who would spend the rest of her days alone. She selflessly let go of her cherished husband so he (and, eventually, his body) could be with his Serbian family. What keeps me going today is that it was her decision to part with him. For that, I will be forever grateful to her.

As we were getting a bit late to catch the plane to Belgrade, we were ushered through the passport control. By then I was in pieces myself and could not hide my sorrow. I just cried and cried discreetly until we got onto the plane and sat down.

My brother was very ill; probably too weak and sick to travel. I was worried he might not make the three-hour journey to Serbia. That flight seemed to last an eternity.

When we got to Belgrade, his son was waiting for us. We took him straight to the best oncology clinic. We hoped that they would admit him and make him as comfortable as possible with medication. Instead, the oncologist examined him and gave us more bad news. The doctor lifted up my brother's shirt and saw something like two small chicken eggs joined together. The growth looked inflamed and gruesome. I could see the expression on the doctor's face when he came away from my brother into another room where he explained to his son about the seriousness of his father's illness.

The doctor said, 'I deal with many cancer patients, but I have never seen anything like what I just saw on your father. I'm sorry to tell you that his cancer has spread all over his body. It's just matter of time, and not very much time, before the inevitable happens. I would suggest you consider putting your father in hospice here in Belgrade, so he can be made as comfortable as possible until the end.'

Srecko was devastated. He took a deep breath, then he asked me, 'What do you think? Should we put Dad in hospice?'

It was my turn to take a deep breath. 'Srecko, I made many choices for your father while in Russia and until now. But I think you are the one who should be taking over these kinds of decisions. I'll support you and my brother financially, but you need to decide whether to leave him in the hospice here in Belgrade. Whatever decision you make, I'll stand by you. Just remember that he will be more than 200km from rest of the family.'

My brother left Serbia years ago as I did and for the same reasons: to do better for himself and provide for Mum and Dad and, eventually, his own family. He always supported his son financially and visited him in Serbia whenever he could. When Srecko found out that his father had cancer and how ill he was, he was devastated.

Srecko must have been thinking of how much his father had done for him when he told me his decision. 'It's time for payback. I'm ready to take my father back home where he belongs –with me, his three grandchildren and the rest of the family – for the remaining time that he has left to live so everyone can visit him. My wife and I will look after him.

'Okay. 'I nodded and patted his back.

Before we started our 200-km journey back home, my brother was given morphine for his constant, unbearable pain. It was heart-breaking for his son and me to watch Zivoslav suffer so much.

The next day, we arrived at his son's house. We took my brother to the best oncology doctors to prescribe him the right medication to minimise his pain as much as possible. I also paid for private nursing care to look after my brother at home. There wasn't anything more I could have done for him before returning to the UK. I stayed for two more weeks and will never forget how my brother rallied for one week. No one would have known that he was ill while I was there. He was laughing, joking and enjoyed playing with his young grandchildren.

I took many pictures of him with his family that I will treasure for years to come. My brother was always a positive, uplifting person. And his optimism remained with him to the very end. He insisted daily that the lumps on his chest be removed, never accepting that he was too ill for a full recovery.

Zivoslav was in daily contact with his wife in Russia. They kept telling each other how much they loved each other. I overheard many conversations when Zivoslav would tell his wife, 'Don't cry! I am feeling much better, and as soon as they operate on my chest and I get stronger, I will be back to work and earn loads of money for us. I might even help Srecko finish his house over here in Serbia. But don't worry, I will look after you. I promise. I love you. I love you with all my heart. Stay strong, Katia.'

It was excruciating for me and rest of the family to hear my brother telling us that he couldn't wait to go back to his wife and go back to work. We all went along with his plans as we didn't want to upset him, discourage him or cause him any more pain than he was already in, but it was hard for me to play along. I was lying to him.

The day before I returned to the UK, my brother said, 'You'll be getting married to David in four weeks' time. Good luck, and I wish you and David all the happiness in the world. Please remember that, whatever happens to me, you must go ahead with your wedding day; it's your future. God bless you both.'

I told my nephew that I had done my best for my brother, and if anything happened the day before or on the day of my wedding, not to let me know. 'I won't be able to come back for his funeral, and your dad wants me to have a happy wedding day.' I gave Srecko a sad smile and told him, 'I'll call after the wedding to see how he's doing.'

Srecko nodded. 'Okay.'

The day I left Serbia, my brother thanked me for all my support and for bringing him back to his son and grandchildren. It was satisfying and rewarding for me to hear him saying so. I rest a bit easier knowing that his Serbian family can visit his grave whenever they wish to. If my brother had died and had been buried in Russia, none of his family would have been able to afford to visit his grave regularly. We said our goodbyes and sobbed our hearts out as we knew that we were not going to see each other again. Then I left.

Chapter 25

Endings and Beginnings

My fiancé, Dave, and I went out for dinner the night before we got married. We ordered our food, and then I received a text message on my mobile from my brother's friend, Ivan, in Russia saying, 'Please accept my condolences for my dear friend Zivoslav and your brother who is not with us anymore.'

As I already knew, I called one of my sisters, and she said, 'As you know our brother must be buried tomorrow. I am so sorry it will be on your wedding day. 'We both cried.

Everything for the wedding was booked and sorted out. I had a blessing from my brother that he wanted me to go ahead with the wedding. And we did. Dave and I agreed not to tell anyone until the day after the wedding.

On my wedding day, I went to my hairdresser, came back, got dressed for the wedding and I mumbled to myself, 'Come on, you can do it. You are marrying the man of your dreams, and your son is giving you away. Just keep calm and don't let anyone see you unhappy. 'I was able to manage through the day and even enjoy myself, but it was a trying day for me. This time around (for different reasons) some of my family members were there, but my brother was buried on my wedding day. That fact would cast a shadow on anyone's celebration; it certainly did on mine.

We didn't have a fancy wedding. We got married in a registry office with close family and friends present. When we booked our wedding, we got some brilliant advice from the kind and thoughtful registrar. She suggested that our wedding should be as special as possible, even though it was a registry office affair between two older people who had been married before. One of her ideas was to have our guests be seated before I enter with my son. I liked that. I asked my son to give me away and was delighted that he agreed. My darling son, David, has been my centre, my purpose, my inspiration, my everything since he was born. I am proud of him and love him dearly. I wouldn't have felt right if he hadn't been a part of that significant day in my life.

Just before we made our way in, I could hear the registrar's announcement saying, 'Please be upstanding to welcome the bride under her son's arm.' When I heard those words, I was the proudest and happiest mum on the planet. I was able to walk in with my son, David, who gave me away to my future husband, David.

The wedding of my dreams. I was over the moon with my darling boy escorting me to marry my beloved Dave. And Zivoslav was with me in spirit.

My heart was bursting with love and joy when I kept my focus on my two Davids. But all I had to do was to look at anyone in my family to snap me back to the overwhelming grief that weighed down my heart. My dear, dead brother was being buried more or less at the same time as I was getting married. What I thought at the time was, *my brother should be with me right now at my wedding, so I can be entirely happy. But, I know he's with me all the way in spirit. I must remember that.*

When I walked in, I saw my Dave standing there, waiting for me and looking as dapper as when we had our first date fifteen years ago. I was shaking with happiness when I was handed over from one David to another. What a magnificent feeling that was. I felt as if the bright and shiny life I always hoped for was beginning, and I tried hard not to let the end of my brother's life dim the glow of the moment. It was an exhilarating and exhausting and unforgettable day.

Unlike my first wedding photo, I'm clearly smiling.

The wedding reception was lovely, and everyone was happy, including Dave and me. As we were dancing cheek-to-cheek, he whispered in my ear. 'For two old-timers, we still look pretty good, don't you think, Darling?'

I smiled and raised my head so I could look directly into his loving eyes. Tears welled up in my eyes. I playfully tipped my head as single tear gently rolled down my cheek. Before I could wipe it away, he did. I put my hand over his and said, 'Old-timers? Not us, Darling. All I see are two hearts, both a little wounded from what life has thrown our way, but both still open and strong enough to love...well, wholeheartedly.'

Dave raised an eyebrow, and we both began to laugh. It felt magnificent, overdue, and most importantly, healing.

Author Biography

Dee Shaw lives in England with her darling husband, Dave. Her life continues to be a journey celebrated by many blessings and daunted with heart-breaking trials. *Life is a Gamble* is her first book but hopefully not her last.